NATIONAL
GEOGRAPHIC
KiDS

ALMANAC
2020

A red panda eats bamboo in Wolong National Nature Reserve in Sichuan Province, China.

NATIONAL GEOGRAPHIC KiDS

ALMANAC
2020

NATIONAL GEOGRAPHIC
WASHINGTON, D.C.

National Geographic Kids Books
gratefully acknowledges the following people for their help with the
National Geographic Kids Almanac.

Jennifer Leff of the National Geographic Explorer Programs

Amazing Animals

Suzanne Braden, Director, Pandas International

Dr. Rodolfo Coria, Paleontologist, Plaza Huincul, Argentina

Dr. Sylvia Earle, National Geographic Explorer-in-Residence

Dr. Thomas R. Holtz, Jr., Senior Lecturer, Vertebrate Paleontology, Department of Geology, University of Maryland

Dr. Luke Hunter, Executive Director, Panthera

Dereck and Beverly Joubert, National Geographic Explorers-in-Residence

Nizar Ibrahim, National Geographic Explorer

"Dino" Don Lessem, President, Exhibits Rex

Kathy B. Maher, Research Editor (former), National Geographic magazine

Kathleen Martin, Canadian Sea Turtle Network

Barbara Nielsen, Polar Bears International

Andy Prince, Austin Zoo

Julia Thorson, translator, Zurich, Switzerland

Dennis vanEngelsdorp, Senior Extension Associate, Pennsylvania Department of Agriculture

Science and Technology
Space and Earth

Tim Appenzeller, Chief Magazine Editor, Nature

Dr. Rick Fienberg, American Astronomical Society, Press Officer and Director of Communications

Dr. José de Ondarza, Associate Professor, Department of Biological Sciences, State University of New York, College at Plattsburgh

Lesley B. Rogers, Managing Editor (former), National Geographic magazine

Dr. Enric Sala, National Geographic Explorer-in-Residence

Abigail A. Tipton, Director of Research (former), National Geographic magazine

Erin Vintinner, Biodiversity Specialist, Center for Biodiversity and Conservation at the American Museum of Natural History

Barbara L. Wyckoff, Research Editor (former), National Geographic magazine

Going Green

Eric J. Bohn, Math Teacher, Santa Rosa High School

Stephen David Harris, Professional Engineer, Industry Consulting

Catherine C. Milbourn, Senior Press Officer, EPA

Brad Scriber, Senior Researcher, National Geographic magazine

Paola Segura and Cid Simões, National Geographic Emerging Explorers

Dr. Wes Tunnell, Harte Research Institute for Gulf of Mexico Studies, Texas A&M University–Corpus Christi

Natasha Vizcarra, Science Writer and Media Liaison, National Snow and Ice Data Center

Culture Connection

Dr. Wade Davis, National Geographic Explorer-in-Residence

Deirdre Mullervy, Managing Editor, Gallaudet University Press

Wonders of Nature

Anatta, NOAA Public Affairs Officer

Dr. Robert Ballard, National Geographic Explorer-in-Residence

Douglas H. Chadwick, wildlife biologist and contributor to National Geographic magazine

Susan K. Pell, Ph.D., Science and Public Programs Manager, United States Botanic Garden

History Happens

Dr. Sylvie Beaudreau, Associate Professor, Department of History, State University of New York

Elspeth Deir, Assistant Professor, Faculty of Education, Queens University, Kingston, Ontario, Canada

Dr. Gregory Geddes, Professor, Global Studies, State University of New York–Orange, Middletown-Newburgh, New York

Dr. Fredrik Hiebert, National Geographic Visiting Fellow

Micheline Joanisse, Media Relations Officer, Natural Resources Canada

Dr. Robert D. Johnston, Associate Professor and Director of the Teaching of History Program, University of Illinois at Chicago

Dickson Mansfield, Geography Instructor (retired), Faculty of Education, Queens University, Kingston, Ontario, Canada

Tina Norris, U.S. Census Bureau

Parliamentary Information and Research Service, Library of Parliament, Ottawa, Canada

Karyn Pugliese, Acting Director, Communications, Assembly of First Nations

Geography Rocks

Carl Haub, Senior Demographer, Conrad Taeuber Chair of Public Information, Population Reference Bureau

Dr. Toshiko Kaneda, Senior Research Associate, Population Reference Bureau

Dr. Kristin Bietsch, Research Associate, Population Reference Bureau

Dr. Walt Meier, National Snow and Ice Data Center

Dr. Richard W. Reynolds, NOAA's National Climatic Data Center

United States Census Bureau, Public Help Desk

Contents

Contents

NATIONAL GEOGRAPHIC KIDS

ALMANAC **CHALLENGE** 2020

THE RESULTS ARE IN!

Which lion poster was the favorite in our 2019 online pole? *See page 191.*

Want to become part of the 2020 Almanac Challenge? Go to page 190 to find out more.

YOUR
WORLD
2020

A surfer rides a wave in Fiji. Surfing will make its debut at the 2020 Olympic Games in Tokyo, Japan.

10 WAYS THE WORLD HAS CHANGED SINCE THE 2010 ALMANAC

PANDA BOOM

In 2010, China's Wolong National Nature Reserve was just beginning to rebuild after a devastating earthquake in 2008 that left dozens of pandas homeless. Today, Wolong—home to 10 percent of all living pandas in the world—has been rebuilt, and its breeding program recently welcomed 42 cubs. This panda boom means the beloved animals are now off the endangered list—hopefully for good.

FINAL FLIGHT

In 2010, NASA announced that its 30-year space shuttle program would fly its final mission in 2011. Now, NASA's focus is on exploring Mars, and scientists are using the Mars rovers to search for signs of life—and to determine if humans could one day live on the red planet.

OCEAN AID

Since 2010, large areas of the South Atlantic and South Pacific Oceans have been designated as Marine Protected Areas (MPAs). While only some 4 percent of the world's oceans are now protected from human activities like overfishing, it's a positive step toward saving our seas.

A BIG WORLD

The planet's population is growing—by the billions! It now stands at some 7.6 billion people, nearly a billion more than the population in 2010. And there's no sign of a slowdown: Experts estimate the number to hit 8 billion by 2023.

POWER UP

There were fewer than 17,000 electric cars on the roads around the world in 2010. Today, there are more than 3 million. While this may not mean the end of gas-powered vehicles for good, the electric car count is estimated to hit 125 million by 2030.

TABLET TAKEOVER

Back in 2010 when Apple first introduced the iPad, just about 5 percent of U.S. households owned a tablet. Now? More than half of the nation is tuned into such devices. Worldwide, some 20 percent of the population is on team tablet. But far more—66 percent—stick to smartphones.

POTTER MANIA

Millions of Muggles across the globe flocked to movie theaters in 2010 and 2011 to see *Harry Potter and the Deathly Hallows Part 1* and *Part 2*, the final films in the über-popular series. Today, Harry is as beloved as ever, with the hit play *Harry Potter and the Cursed Child* and several theme parks featuring all things Potter.

LOST AND FOUND

In 2018, the last remaining male northern white rhino passed away, marking a sad blow to this rare subspecies. While some animals' numbers are dwindling, others are just being discovered: Since 2010, scientists have found a walking catfish, a two-legged lizard, and the adorable olinguito (above), a small mammal native to South America.

SEEING THE FUTURE

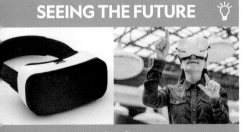

In 2010, virtual reality prototypes were being developed but the tech was not widely available. A decade later, VR is used daily in places like hospitals, classrooms, museums, and in people's homes worldwide.

VIDEO VIEWS

In the past 10 years, YouTube's popularity has exploded. In 2010, some two billion videos were viewed a day. Today? That number exceeds five billion. One of 2010's most popular clips—a man emotionally showing off a double rainbow in his front yard—has been viewed nearly 50 million times since it was originally posted.

GOLDEN GATHERING

BOW, WOW: THIS CELEBRATION HAS GONE TO THE DOGS!

In 2018, the Golden Retriever Club of Scotland welcomed 361 golden retrievers from around the world to an estate in the Scottish Highlands. The occasion? The 150th birthday of the very first litter of golden retrievers, born in July 1868. Golden retrievers were originally bred by a Scottish politician and businessman known as Lord Tweedmouth to be hunting companions that could also swim far distances. Today, golden retrievers rank among the world's most popular and beloved dog breeds, paws down.

ICY MAZE

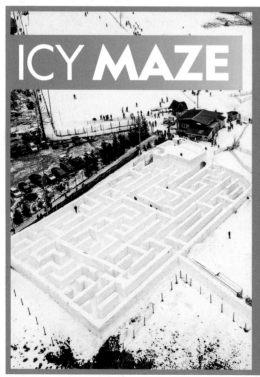

THIS LABYRINTH IN POLAND

is nothing short of a-*maze*-ing! Constructed out of some 60,000 individual blocks of ice and snow, the maze at Snowlandia Zakopane Park covers an area that's about the size of five basketball courts. Each winter, it takes some 50 workers about one month to build the maze, which features narrow passages with walls taller than most adults. And if you find your way out with time to spare, Snowlandia also offers its visitors a chance to explore a five-story snow castle, complete with an icy throne. Talk about some *royal* fun!

Olympic Fever

TOKYO 2020
TOKYO
TOKYO 2020

IN THE SUMMER OF 2020,

Tokyo will become the first Asian city to become a repeat host of the Summer Olympics, having welcomed the games to the Japanese capital in 1964. When the 32nd Olympic Games kick off on July 24, 2020, millions of ticket holders will watch athletes from around the world compete in 33 different sports. Which events are new this year? Women's softball and men's baseball are back on the program after being removed in 2008, and karate, sport climbing, surfing, and skateboarding will be competed on the Olympic stage for the first time ever. So even more athletes will have a chance to go for the gold.

> Hey, would you mind scratching my back while we're up here?

Team Canada competes in Team Synchronized Swimming at the London 2012 Olympic Games.

Team USA basketball players Kevin Durant and DeAndre Jordan joke on the podium after receiving gold medals at the Rio 2016 Olympic Games.

> I can't believe I forgot to wish my mom a happy birthday ...

Meet Miraitowa and Someity, the official mascots of the 2020 Olympics and Paralympic Games! Selected by elementary school children throughout Japan, the cheerful mascots are named for the Japanese words for future and eternity (Miraitowa) and mighty (Someity). Together, the mascots are meant to represent both tradition and innovation.

Real-Life TRANSFORMERS

When it comes to some robots, there's more than meets the eye!

Modeled after the popular Transformers toys, the J-deite RIDE robot is programmed to shift into a car and back to a bot again. The robot, which was designed by a team of Japanese engineers, is taller than an elephant and weighs about the same as a rhino. In about one minute, it can switch from a robot to a drivable car that seats two. As for its top speed on the roads? The J-deite RIDE top speeds of 37 miles an hour (60 km/h).

Hit a switch on a remote control and the J-deite RIDE returns to its robot form. While upright, it can walk about 328 feet (100 m) an hour. That pace is not nearly as speedy as the fictional Transformers, but it's not too bad for a real-life robot!

HOT MOVIES in 2020*

- *Trolls World Tour*
- *Barbie*
- *Peter Rabbit 2*
- *Minions 2*
- *The Croods 2*
- *Sing 2*
- *The SpongeBob Movie: It's a Wonderful Sponge*

*Release dates and titles are subject to change.

Walking Gorilla

WHEN LOUIS THE GORILLA wants to get around his habitat at the Philadelphia Zoo, he doesn't always move about on all fours like most apes. Instead, he walks on his own two feet, completely upright!

The strange sight is super uncommon for gorillas, who typically walk on two legs once in a while, and just for a few seconds. But six-foot (1.8-m)-tall Louis is seen standing quite often, taking quick strides across the yards, just like a human.

So why does Louis love to walk? Researchers who work with him at the Philadelphia Zoo say it has to do with his preference for keeping his hands clean. He walks when he's gathering food like tomatoes, leading experts to think that he doesn't want to crush the juicy snacks by walking on his hands. Louis also stands up and walks when his yard is muddy, and he has been seen using leaves to wipe dirt off his hands and feet. Sounds like Louis is one particular primate!

THERE ARE TORNADOES ... AND THEN THERE ARE *LAVANADOES.*

KILAUEA'S STRANGE PHENOMENON

A lavanado happens when a funnel forms over an active volcano, forming a twister of fire, smoke, ash, and, yes, even lava if it can stay suspended in the air. Recently, a lavanado was spotted over Kilauea on Hawaii's Big Island, the result of intense heat and high winds rising rapidly from the raging volcano. This terrifying twister, measuring some 200 feet (61 m) long, could be spotted whirling over the island from half a mile (800 m) away. Similar columns have been seen over large wildfires, also forming from a combination of high heat and wind.

While lavanadoes are rare, they are fascinating examples of the extreme weather produced around active volcanoes—and proof of just how powerful these forces of nature truly are.

Cool Events 2020

GILROY GARLIC FESTIVAL

Garlic ice cream? Why not!
That's just one of the fun foods found at this festival showcasing the smelly veggie in northern California, U.S.A.

July 24–July 26

POLAR BEAR SWIM

100 years have passed since the first people plunged into the icy waters near Vancouver, Canada. Today, thousands of brave swimmers jump right into this New Year tradition.

January 1

SUMMER PARALYMPIC GAMES

LET THE GAMES BEGIN!
Thousands of athletes with various disabilities head to Tokyo.

August 25–September 6

WORLD FROG DAY

Ribbit, ribbit! Show your love for these hopping amphibians today.

March 20

WORLD SMILE DAY

SAY CHEESE!
Today, you've got plenty to grin about!

October 2

EARTH DAY

The **50TH ANNIVERSARY OF THIS EVENT** reminds us to protect the planet today—and every day.

April 22

MAYFLOWER VOYAGE

400TH ANNIVERSARY
It has been four centuries since the *Mayflower* brought the Pilgrims from England to America.

November

WORLD OCEAN DAY

Celebrate the seas and all of the living things that call our oceans home.

June 8

ROLL ON

As part of a Christmas Eve custom, the locals of Caracas, Venezuela, lace up their roller skates and glide to church.

December 24

ESCAPE ROOM

The lights turn off, and there you are: In a dark, windowless room, with your friends and family ... and no way out. Sound like the start of a scary movie? Not quite. You are in an escape room—and it's all for fun!

Escape rooms, which first started in Tokyo in 2007, have been popping up all around the world as a family-friendly activity. The concept is simple: Your group is locked in a room and is given about an hour to search for clues and solve puzzles to figure out how to exit. Cracking the code is all about teamwork and plenty of problem-solving. Escape rooms have become so popular that there is even an adventure park in Budapest, Hungary, where you can spend an entire day attempting to get out by conquering a series of physical and mental obstacles.

And if you don't crack the code in an escape room? It's okay! You still get to leave the room—and you're always welcome to come back for escape room redemption.

A Not-So-Great Escape!

While most people try to break out of an escape room, one harebrained burglar in Vancouver, Washington, U.S.A., went the opposite route. After breaking into an escape room (where he allegedly ate a burrito he brought with him and pocketed a remote control and a cell phone), the bad guy began to worry he couldn't actually, uh, escape. Scared, he called 911. And even though he eventually found an exit, the cops still busted him for burglary.

HIGH-TECH TEACHER

ROBOTS CAN DO JUST ABOUT ANYTHING THESE DAYS.

Including teach a class full of kids! At least that's what Elias the robot is doing in Finland. As part of a test program, Elias and three other humanoid robots are

programmed to work with students to teach subjects like math and language. He can speak 23 languages, ask questions, and even give feedback on the kids to human teachers. But Elias isn't just about reading and writing. He can break out some serious dance moves! Sounds like one rockin' robot.

A panther chameleon flashes a threat display in Masoala National Park, Madagascar.

AMAZING ANIMALS

EARTH EXPLORER

Meet **Krithi Karanth!**

This conservation biologist and National Geographic explorer is hoping to solve conflict between wildlife and humans in her home country, India.

From the time she was a kid, Krithi Karanth has been concerned about the need to protect wildlife. In fact, as the daughter of a conservationist, Krithi spotted her first tiger and leopard in the wild when she was just two years old. Today, as a conservation scientist, Krithi is focused on keeping the wildlife in her native India around for future generations.

One way she's doing just that? By trying to limit the conflict between farmers throughout the many villages in India and the wildlife that often wind up on their land. These animals—including feral pigs, tigers, leopards, and elephants—crush crops, mangle fences, and even harm farm animals.

"Spaces for wildlife are shrinking, and people are in closer contact with wildlife," explains Krithi. "As a result, the frustrated and sometimes furious farmers chase or harm animals."

Krithi is working to build tolerance by helping people report and get paid by the government for damage caused by wild animals. She created Wild Seve, a phone reporting system through which people in the field file reports of damage for farmers. Once a report is filed, the farmer receives payment for their losses from the Indian government.

"If farmers are covered for their loss, they will be less likely to retaliate," explains Krithi. She hopes this simple system will be a way to keep humans happy—and animals alive.

Krithi is also intent on raising awareness of India's unique wildlife to the rest of the world. She has even written her own children's book called *Will You Play With Me?* to introduce kids to animals found only in India—like the lion-tailed macaque and the wild dog—and to get kids excited about and to value the animals found in their own countries.

"It's easy to think that all of the discoveries have been done and the species have all been found, but that's not true," says Karanth. "There is still a lot of exploration left to do."

Female Asian elephants don't have tusks.

ASIAN ELEPHANTS

" The big question we have to ask in India is, 'Is there room for wildlife?' And the answer has to be yes. "

BENGAL TIGER

No two tigers have the same pattern of stripes.

CALL TO ACTION!

Pick a cause—whether it's saving big cats or boosting the bee population—and look into the ways you can support it. "You don't have to sit back and say 'I can't do anything,'" says Krithi. "Go out and learn everything you can about wildlife. Take pictures of animals and write about them." Who knows, maybe one day you'll play a major role in saving a species.

Extraordinary ANIMALS

KITTEN on WHEELS

I rock ... and roll.

Fort Langley, Canada
When the TinyKittens Society found a starving kitten suffering from a terrible injury to his back legs, they were shocked he was still alive. But his rescuers refused to give up on him. After amputating part of the cat's back legs, his medical team constructed slings, splints, and eventually a set of mini wheels to give his back end a lift and keep him mobile.

Throughout the process, the team documented the cat's progress on social media. He had tons of fans! Nobody would have guessed that after seven months of intensive physical therapy, the miracle cat—now called Cassidy—would be able to get around without the help of his wheels. These days he scoots around on his two front paws. Except when he's tired, of course—then he hitches a ride on his new family's robotic vacuum cleaner.

CASSIDY NO LONGER NEEDS WHEELS TO GET AROUND.

"Hoppy" to see me?

TOADZILLA!

Darwin, Australia
In the dark of night, a group of citizens set out to hunt down one of Australia's most menacing predators. Their prey? A giant toad nicknamed Toadzilla.

Looking like a cantaloupe with legs, Toadzilla is the largest cane toad on record in Australia, at about eight inches (20.3 cm) long and almost two pounds (0.9 kg). Why the toad hunt? Cane toads were brought to Australia all the way from Hawaii to eat crop-destroying beetles, but instead they gobble down just about anything they can get their mouths around. "Cane toads take away food from other predators and are killing many other native animals," says Graeme Sawyer of FrogWatch, which leads expeditions such as the one that netted Toadzilla.

Luckily cane toads are slow and easy to catch. Once Sawyer's team heard Toadzilla's distinctive mating call—"like a dial tone on a telephone," he says—a tracker grabbed the creature by hand.

Now instead of being a predator, Toadzilla is a teacher, visiting schools to educate kids about invasive species like the cane toad. Better listen to *this* teacher!

TOADZILLA, A GIANT CANE TOAD, IS HANDLED BY THE TRACKER WHO LOCATED THE CREATURE.

The birds ALL call me for fashion tips.

PARROT wears SWEATERS

Lecompton, Kansas

Chilly temperatures never get Javi the bird down. That's because the lesser sulphur-crested cockatoo (a type of parrot) owns plenty of sweaters to keep herself warm!

Normally birds rely on their feathers to stay toasty. But Javi—who was likely raised in harsh conditions before moving to the Tallgrass Parrot Sanctuary—probably plucked out most of her feathers because of stress. Caretakers weren't sure if her belly and chest feathers would grow back, but they knew Javi would be more comfortable with another layer covering her delicate skin. So they fitted her with a sweater.

Today the cockatoo owns more than 20 sweaters. They're made from colorful socks that Tallgrass co-owner Kail Marie makes herself. The fashions have caught the eye of Javi's bird friends, Sassy and Poppy. "Javi's the leader," Marie says. "They'll follow her anywhere." Looks like Javi got more than a new wardrobe—she got new friends as well.

PUPPIES save LOST BOY

Virgilina, Virginia

Jaylynn Thorpe's family was terrified when the three-year-old wandered off into the woods on a frigid 17°F (-8.3°C) night. Thankfully, Bootsy and Dipstick the puppies wandered off with him—and probably saved his life.

While rescue workers searched for Jaylynn with scent-sniffing dogs and a heat-seeking helicopter, the puppies nestled around the shivering boy. They pressed against him all night and kept him warm—and alive. "They treated him like another puppy in their litter," veterinarian Emily Kinnaird says. "They snuggled to keep warm."

Twenty hours later, rescuers were nearby. But a scared Jaylynn hid beneath a pile of leaves. Once again, the puppies played the heroes, barking to alert the rescue team. Jaylynn was reunited with his family, cold and hungry but unhurt. "The puppies were very important to his survival," fire chief Chad Loftis says.

Here we come to save the day!

RADIO FLYER

BOOTSY (LEFT) AND DIPSTICK

INCREDIBLE ANIMAL FRIENDS

I love ya, but I think your coat needs washing.

DOMESTIC GOOSE

ORIGIN Europe and Asia
WEIGHT 5 to 10 pounds (2.3 to 4.5 kg)
CLAIM TO FAME The goose is thought to be one of the first animals to be domesticated, probably in Egypt about 3,000 years ago.
FUN TO KNOW The wing-span of a domestic goose can be six feet (1.8 m) wide.

Step away from the bull!

HIGHLAND BULL

ORIGIN Scotland; these bulls were brought to Australia (near New Zealand) by Scottish immigrants
WEIGHT 1,500 to 1,800 pounds (680.4 to 816.5 kg)
CLAIM TO FAME Highland cattle grow two coats of hair. The coarse outer layer protects the animals from wind and rain, and the soft bottom layer keeps them warm.
FUN TO KNOW Experts think Highland cattle have been around since the sixth century.

GOOSE GUARDS BULL

GISBORNE, NEW ZEALAND

A big Highland bull like Hamish probably doesn't need a bodyguard, but this goose disagrees. Whenever the bull is grazing in the pasture, the goose watches for cattle that—in the bird's opinion—get way too close. "Then the goose will stretch out his neck, shriek, and chase the other cows and bulls away," says Kees Weytsmans, owner of the Knapdale Eco Lodge where the two live.

Hamish and the goose have been inseparable for 10 years—ever since the bird was found resting on Hamish's leg a week after the bull was born. Since then, the goose has rarely left Hamish's side. Weytsmans once moved Hamish to another rancher's pasture for a few nights. But one evening apart was all the goose could stand. "The next afternoon the goose traveled all by himself to the other pasture to find Hamish," he says. And though Hamish doesn't seem as eager for friendship as the goose, the bull doesn't mind his bodyguard. Otherwise, this bull would ruffle some feathers!

MONKEY DOTES ON IGUANA

KREFELD, GERMANY

This white-faced saki rarely scaled back her affection for her green iguana bestie. The saki, a type of monkey, loved petting and snuggling her reptile pal as they lounged together on tree branches at the Krefeld Zoo.

The saki and iguana met after they were placed in the zoo's Rain Forest House, a tree-filled enclosure that's home to 40 different types of animals from tropical areas. "Both green iguanas and white-faced sakis spend most of their time in treetops," zoo spokesperson Petra Schwinn says. "One day these two crossed paths." The curious saki examined the reptile, patting its skin with her long fingers.

The pals continued to have hangout sessions, eating together at the enclosure's feeding station. But most of their "playdates" were in the trees and involved the saki petting the iguana and tickling his chin. The reptile, meanwhile, seemed to soak up the attention.

Recently the animals moved to separate zoos. But keepers and visitors haven't forgotten about their friendship. "They made a good team," Schwinn says.

THE FEMALE SAKI PETS HER IGUANA PAL.

GREEN IGUANA

RANGE
Central and South America

WEIGHT
11 pounds (5 kg)

TALL TAIL
If it's caught by a predator, the green iguana can detach its tail and grow another.

FUNNY NAME
These animals are sometimes referred to as "bamboo chickens."

Hey, your beard feels a bit sharp. How about a shave?

WHITE-FACED SAKI

RANGE
South America

WEIGHT
around 4 pounds (1.8 kg)

FACE OFF
Only male white-faced sakis have white fur covering their faces. The fur on a female's face is mostly brown.

SWEET TREATS
Sakis eat fruit, honey, leaves, and flowers.

25

WHAT IS Taxonomy?

Since there are billions and billions of living things, called organisms, on the planet, people need a way of classifying them. Scientists created a system called **taxonomy,** which helps to classify all living things into ordered groups. By putting organisms into categories, we are better able to understand how they are the same and how they are different. There are eight levels of taxonomic classification, beginning with the broadest group, called a domain, followed by kingdom, down to the most specific group, called a species.

Biologists divide life based on evolutionary history, and they place organisms into three domains depending on their genetic structure: Archaea, Bacteria, and Eukarya. (See p. 85 for "The Three Domains of Life.")

Where do animals come in?

Animals are a part of the Eukarya domain, which means they are organisms made of cells with nuclei. More than one million species of animals have been named, including humans. Like all living things, animals can be divided into smaller groups, called phyla. Most scientists believe there are more than 30 phyla into which animals can be grouped based on certain scientific criteria, such as body type or whether or not the animal has a backbone. It can be pretty complicated, so there is another, less complicated system that groups animals into two categories: vertebrates and invertebrates.

HEDGEHOG

SAMPLE CLASSIFICATION
KEEL-BILLED TOUCAN

Domain:	Eukarya
Kingdom:	Animalia
Phylum:	Chordata
Class:	Aves
Order:	Piciformes
Family:	Ramphastidae
Genus:	Ramphastos
Species:	sulfuratus

TIP:
Here's a sentence to help you remember the classification order:
Did **K**ing **P**hillip **C**ome **O**ver **F**or **G**ood **S**oup?

BY THE NUMBERS

There are 13,267 vulnerable or endangered animal species in the world. The list includes:

• 1,204 mammals, such as the snow leopard, the polar bear, and the fishing cat.

• 1,469 birds, including the Steller's sea eagle and the black-banded plover.

• 2,386 fish, such as the Mekong giant catfish.

• 1,215 reptiles, including the American crocodile.

• 1,414 insects, including the Macedonian grayling.

• 2,100 amphibians, such as the Round Island day gecko.

• And more, including 170 arachnids, 732 crustaceans, 239 sea anemones and corals, 190 bivalves, and 1,992 snails and slugs.

ROUND ISLAND DAY GECKO

Vertebrates
Animals WITH Backbones

Fish are cold-blooded and live in water. They breathe with gills, lay eggs, and usually have scales.

Amphibians are cold-blooded. Their young live in water and breathe with gills. Adults live on land and breathe with lungs.

Reptiles are cold-blooded and breathe with lungs. They live both on land and in water.

Birds are warm-blooded and have feathers and wings. They lay eggs, breathe with lungs, and usually are able to fly. Some birds live on land, some in water, and some on both.

Mammals are warm-blooded and feed on their mothers' milk. They also have skin that is usually covered with hair. Mammals live both on land and in water.

BIRD: MANDARIN DUCK

AMPHIBIAN: POISON DART FROG

Invertebrates
Animals WITHOUT Backbones

Sponges are a very basic form of animal life. They live in water and do not move on their own.

Echinoderms have external skeletons and live in seawater.

Mollusks have soft bodies and can live either in or out of shells, on land or in water.

Arthropods are the largest group of animals. They have external skeletons, called exoskeletons, and segmented bodies with appendages. Arthropods live in water and on land.

Worms are soft-bodied animals with no true legs. Worms live in soil.

Cnidaria live in water and have mouths surrounded by tentacles.

MOLLUSK: MAGNIFICENT CHROMODORID NUDIBRANCH

SPONGE: SEA SPONGE

Cold-blooded
versus
Warm-blooded

Cold-blooded animals, also called ectotherms, get their heat from outside their bodies.

Warm-blooded animals, also called endotherms, keep their body temperature level regardless of the temperature of their environment.

GARDEN SNAIL

27

RISE OF THE TIGER

An adult male tiger can weigh the same as eight 10-year-old kids.

Tigers live in both cold and hot climates.

Scientists find good news with the help of secret snaps.

Recently, scientists have worked to get a current global estimate of how many wild tigers exist. As part of the effort, experts in countries throughout the tiger's range, including Russia, Bangladesh, Bhutan, India, and Nepal, trekked to forests and grasslands where the cats live to set up camera traps—motion-sensing or remote-controlled cameras that snap wildlife pics. They hoped the photos would give clues about the number of tigers in each nation.

Cats on Camera

To track down tigers, researchers focused on water holes and areas with boar and other tiger prey. There, they fixed multiple camera traps to trees to catch the cats from different angles. The camera's treelike disguise made them less likely to be destroyed by curious animals. After setting up the traps, the researchers journeyed home.

Take a Number

The cameras snapped pictures of any animal that walked in front of them, using night vision to get good photos in the dark, when tigers are most active. The researchers returned to collect the devices a few months later and uploaded their pictures to computers, which analyzed each tiger's coat pattern and recognized when a certain tiger appeared more than once. The computers then counted how many individuals appeared overall in the photos.

Using this data and other information, teams were able to estimate how many tigers lived in the countries studied. The final tally surprised them all.

Tiger Time

Researchers estimated that about 3,890 wild tigers exist on the planet. That's up from as few as 3,200, the estimated population in 2010. Experts say this bump may be partly due to conservation efforts made by several of the countries where tigers live, such as laws to protect the cats' habitats.

Still, experts emphasize that the rise in numbers doesn't mean that tigers are out of danger. In fact it's possible that better technology may have allowed researchers to photograph more tigers than before, making it seem as if the population is increasing. Still, analyzing these "selfies" is certainly a step in the right direction for the future of wild tigers.

A TIGER CUB INVESTIGATES A CAMERA THAT'S MOUNTED ON WHEELS AND CONTROLLED REMOTELY BY A RESEARCHER.

MARGAYS: OUT ON A LIMB

Meet the margays! These small wild cats, about the size of a house cat, are native to rain forests of Central and South America. Because of their secretive lifestyle—they spend a lot of their lives in trees, even hunting among the branches—catching a glimpse of these acrobatic cats in their natural habitat is no easy task.

BUILT TO CLIMB
With a body uniquely adapted to life in the treetops, a margay moves through the canopy like a feline gymnast. Unlike most wild cats, they can go down a tree headfirst. The margay's ankles can rotate all the way around to face backward, which allows the cat to quickly change direction while climbing.

A margay's feet are wide and soft, with flexible toes that allow it to grab branches. Its 17-inch (43-cm)-long tail provides balance as it moves around in the treetops.

TRACKING MARGAYS
Because they can stay hidden in the trees, experts use radio collars to track these cats and shed some light on their daily activities. As a result, the margay's characteristics and habits aren't a complete secret. Experts have observed that these solitary animals are active mostly at night (their huge eyes help them see in the dark), hunting for birds, snakes, rodents, and even small monkeys. It takes skillful climbing to accomplish that hunting feat.

SAVING MARGAY HABITAT
Though the overall margay population isn't in immediate danger, the cats are vulnerable. Margays need tropical forests to survive. Habitat destruction, especially clearing forests for farms and ranches, is their biggest threat. Today, scientists are working hard to save the habitat of these acrobats of the rain forest.

Climbing skills make margays the acrobats of the rain forest.

CLIMBING HEADFIRST DOWN A TREE IS A RARE ABILITY MARGAYS HAVE MASTERED.

TURBO-CHEETAH

A cheetah can cover 26 feet (8 m) in one stride.

SCIENTISTS USE CUTTING-EDGE TECHNOLOGY TO UNCOVER THE CHEETAH'S BIG SECRET.

The fastest land animal, cheetahs have been clocked going over 60 miles an hour (97 km/h). Naturally, scientists have attributed the cheetah's hunting success to its speediness—until recently. Using top-notch technology to research the feline's movements and hunting techniques, scientists found surprising answers to the question of what makes the cheetah a first-rate predator.

CUTTING-EDGE COLLARS

Until recently, people assumed that the animal's swiftness was what allowed it to snag prey so effectively in the wild. But some experts weren't so sure. So one team, led by Alan Wilson, trekked to Botswana, a country in Africa with one of the world's largest cheetah populations, where they encountered several of the cats on grassy terrain. After zapping them with tranquilizer darts, the scientists fitted them each with a special fashion accessory: a tricked-out radio collar to monitor their movements.

Over the next 18 months, the gadgets sensed when each cheetah was running (which meant that it was hunting), then recorded the cat's location and speed. After 367 runs, the scientists began analyzing the data they'd collected. They knew that the cheetahs were chasing prey. If a cat's run ended with quick, jerky movements and then mostly stillness, they could tell that it had wrestled with and taken down its target.

SMOOTH MOVES

Looking at the cats' speed and the paths in which they ran, the scientists realized that it's not just speed that makes the cheetah a talented hunter—it's the animal's ability to slow down quickly and make sharp turns. Take the antelope, which runs in a zigzag in an attempt to lose its pursuer. The study showed that, like the antelope, the cheetah slows down, makes a tight turn, and speeds off in the same direction—all within seconds. This is a skill cheetahs start to develop as cubs, and with claws that act like running cleats and a long tail to keep them balanced, a cheetah's body is built for making difficult hairpin turns.

All of this makes the cheetah a champion predator. And now that researchers are more aware of this feline's hunting habits, the data may help conservationists create nature reserves where cheetahs can thrive.

A cheetah can take four strides in one second.

Collar Connection

The high-tech collars used by Alan Wilson's team had accelerometers to measure increases and decreases in the feline's speed. They also included gyroscopes that could sense when a cheetah twisted or turned to change direction, and GPS to allow the scientists to pinpoint the felines' exact locations on the savanna.

LIONS OF THE KALAHARI DESERT

E yes half-closed against the wind-blasted sand, a sleek, black-and-gold-maned lion (above) strides along a dry riverbed in the Kalahari Desert. He is one of the lions that roam the desolate sand dunes of southern Africa's Kalahari and Namib Deserts. These lions thrive in an intensely hot landscape. They have learned how to go without water for weeks.

Life for a desert lion is very different from life for a lion in the grassy plains of Africa, such as in the Serengeti of Kenya and Tanzania. There, large prides of up to 20 lions spend most of their time together. A pride is very much like a human family.

Fritz Eloff, a scientist who spent 40 years studying the desert lions of the Kalahari, found that desert lions live, on average, in small groups of fewer than six. Family ties are just as strong, but relationships are long-distance. Desert lions often break up into even smaller groups.

BUSY NIGHTS

Life for Kalahari lions is a constant battle against thirst and high temperatures. In summer during the day, the surface temperature of the sand can be 150°F (66°C). That's hot enough to cook an egg.

Not surprisingly, Kalahari lions hunt mostly after the sun has gone down. The big cats usually rest until the middle of the night, waiting for a cool desert wind. Then they spend the rest of the night walking—looking for food.

In the Serengeti, food is very plentiful. Lions rarely have to walk more than a couple of miles before they find a meal. But life in the desert is not so easy. With only a few scattered animals such as porcupines and gemsboks—horse-size antelopes—for prey, desert lions have to walk farther and work harder to catch dinner.

DANGEROUS DINNER

When Kalahari lions do find something to eat, it is usually spiky or dangerous. One out of every three animals they catch is a porcupine. The desert lion's main prey is the gemsbok, which can provide 10 times as much meat as a porcupine. But gemsboks are difficult to bring down; they've been known to kill lions by skewering them on their three-foot (0.9-m)-long, saberlike horns.

Water is scarce in the Kalahari, so the desert lions have to be as resourceful at finding a drink as they are at finding a meal. One hot day, just as a light rain began to fall, Eloff watched two lionesses. Side by side, they licked the raindrops off each other.

These lean, strong lions have amazingly learned to survive, and by cooperating, they manage to thrive in an inhospitable, almost waterless world.

Surprise Party!

Red-eyed tree frogs astonish others with their weird behavior.

Looking for a snack, a 30-inch (76-cm)-long viper slithers down a tree in a steamy rain forest in Central America. Suddenly it sees a tasty-looking, three-inch (7.6-cm)-long red-eyed tree frog resting on a nearby leaf. The reptile lunges forward and snatches up the tiny croaker in its fanged mouth. But the snake's in for a not-so-pleasant surprise—the frog tastes terrible! The snake immediately spits out the amphibian. Landing unharmed on the forest floor, the frog blinks its big red eyes, then hops off to safety.

Red-eyed tree frogs have some features and behaviors that surprise other animals in their rain forest home, as well as the experts who study them. Discover how these jaw-dropping jumpers turn their habitat into one big surprise party.

The red-eyed tree frog oozes stinky, slightly toxic slime through its skin when a predator is near. It also doesn't taste very good!

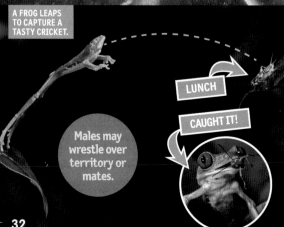

A FROG LEAPS TO CAPTURE A TASTY CRICKET.

LUNCH

CAUGHT IT!

Males may wrestle over territory or mates.

Ambush and Eat

A red-eyed tree frog might jump through the air to get closer to an insect it wants to eat. This animal also uses the element of surprise. Known as an ambush predator, the amphibian sometimes hides among the leaves in its rain forest home. The frog waits patiently until a tasty-looking moth or cricket comes within striking distance. Then it fires out its long, sticky tongue to capture the insect and pull the meal into its mouth. Now *that's* some fast food.

Eye Spy

These nocturnal animals may spend the day lazing on plants, but they can still spy on their habitat. Thanks to a see-through third eyelid

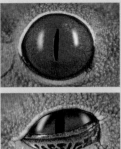

that closes over their eyeballs when resting, the amphibian can stay on the lookout for trouble while it reenergizes. If a hunter does approach, the frog can leap away, startling its pursuer. The eyelid's stripes also may help hide the frog's bright red eyes from would-be predators.

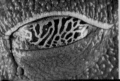

A RED-EYED TREE FROG IN THE COUNTRY OF COSTA RICA SCALES A PLANT SHOOT.

One of the frog's calls sounds like a baby rattle.

Stick to It

Slick surfaces aren't a problem for this frog. It can easily clamber across wet leaves. Instead of hopping, the animal takes careful steps like a pro rock climber. It also has rounded toe pads that stick to surfaces like suction cups, and its feet produce gluey mucus to help it grip slippery surfaces. It can even cling to the undersides of leaves to hide from predators—Spider-Man-style. That's a sticky surprise.

UNDERSIDE OF FOOT

Shake It Off

When researchers visited the country of Panama to study these frogs, they saw something that gave them a jolt: a male frog shaking the shoot of a plant with his hind legs, similar to a person strumming a guitar string! They realized that males do this when other males come too close to their turf. The shaking creates vibrations, which intruders interpret as a signal to back off.

Why not just croak loudly to ward off intruders? "They don't want to reveal their location to the entire pond, including enemies such as frog-eating bats," biologist Michael Caldwell says. That'd shake things up *way* too much.

NORTH AMERICA
ATLANTIC OCEAN
PACIFIC OCEAN
SOUTH AMERICA

Gulf of Mexico

Caribbean Sea

BELIZE
MEXICO
HONDURAS

GUATEMALA
NICARAGUA

EL SALVADOR

COSTA RICA
PANAMA

PACIFIC OCEAN

COLOMBIA

Where red-eyed tree frogs live

33

Meerkat CITY

Meerkats always have something to do. These mongoose relatives live in busy communities, with no time to sit around being bored. In their family groups of up to 40 members, everyone pitches in to get all the jobs done.

Guards

Meerkats are very territorial. Guards, called sentinels, are always on the lookout for rival meerkats that try to move in on their territory. If a sentinel (left) spots any intruding meerkats, it sends out an alarm call. The whole group gathers together and stands tall to try to scare away the rivals. If that doesn't work, meerkats quickly decide whether to fight or retreat.

Predators such as eagles or jackals rate a different warning call. When the sentinel spots a predator, it lets out an alarm call that sends all the meerkats scurrying into the nearest bolt hole—an underground safety den where the eagle can't follow.

A SENTINEL KEEPS WATCH.

Diggers

Picture yourself looking for a tasty bug to eat (below) when suddenly you hear the alarm call for "eagle." You dash left, you dash right, and you finally find a bolt hole.

Bolt holes provide fast getaways for meerkats in danger. Members of the group cooperate to make sure bolt holes are properly dug out, that nothing is blocking the entry, and that there are enough bolt holes in every area.

Meerkats are built to be super diggers. All four of their paws have long, sturdy claws that they use like rakes. They dig to find food, such as lizards and other small reptiles, insects and their larvae, and scorpions.

DIGGING FOR FOOD

Babysitters

Within a meerkat group, the alpha, or leader, female and the alpha male are usually the only ones that have babies. When their babies are too young to follow along while they search for food, meerkat parents have to go without them. So they leave their pups with babysitters—other adult meerkats in the group. The pups stay inside their family's underground burrow for the first three weeks of life, protected and cared for by the babysitters.

HOME SWEET BURROW

WILD DOGS OF AFRICA

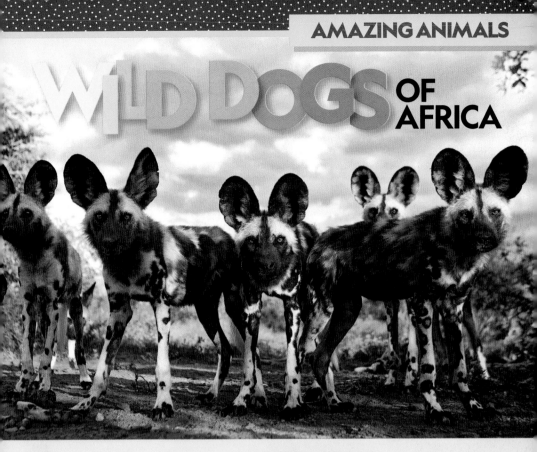

The puppy-dog eyes and pleading squeals of a five-month-old African wild dog named Cici can mean only one thing: dinnertime. An older sister in Cici's pack responds, dragging over a meaty impala bone. In African wild dog society, puppies have all the power. "It's up to the older siblings to take care of the puppies," says Micaela Gunther, a scientist who studies wild dogs, including Cici's family. "The doting grown-ups even deliver toys, such as a strip of impala skin perfect for puppy tug-of-war." Imagine your big brother or sister working hard to hand you snacks and games while you eat, play, and rest all day.

DOG DAYS

Like wolves, wild dogs live in packs of about 15 dogs. Pups stay in the pack for about two years. Then some may break off to start packs of their own, while others stay with their mom and dad.

When the pups are newborn, every member of the pack works together to provide for them. At first the puppies stay near the den, often under the watch of a babysitter, while the pack hunts. Returning pack members throw up meat for the pups. Sound gross? Puppies love these leftovers.

PACK ATTACK

By the time the pups are six months old, they join the pack on hunting expeditions. First they learn how to stalk prey, and eventually they participate in the kill. Single 60-pound (27-kg) dogs rarely catch larger prey on their own, but a pack of 20 proves that there really is strength in numbers. Together they can take down a zebra or wildebeest weighing up to 1,000 pounds (454 kg).

Hunting wild dogs often pursue herds of gazelle for miles, fresh dogs trading places with tired ones. Eventually the weakest of the chased animals tires. The dogs surround it and attack from every direction. This teamwork is bred from the pack's intense social bonding, such as puppy play sessions. Team-building is the reason wild dogs spoil the pups, who grow up united and ready to contribute to the strength of the pack.

SCALY
SUPERHEROES

Discover the hidden powers of the pangolin.

Clark Kent and Peter Parker—the alter egos of Superman and Spider-Man—don't really stand out. And neither do pangolins in the tropical forests or grasslands of Africa and Asia where they live. But like your favorite movie heroes, this animal has a few hidden superpowers. Check them out here.

ASIA
AFRICA
ATLANTIC OCEAN
INDIAN OCEAN
AUSTRALIA
Where pangolins live

SPIDER-MAN STICKINESS!

SPIDER-MAN

Spider-Man shoots out sticky strands of webbing from his wrists to swing from one skyscraper to another. When a pangolin is hungry, it shoots out its sticky tongue, which extends up to 16 inches (40.6 cm) past its mouth. Coated in gluey saliva, the licker scoops up ants and termites, the pangolin's favorite snacks. In all, the mammal can eat some 70 million insects a year. Makes sense that this superhero-like creature would have a super appetite.

WOLVERINE CLAWS!

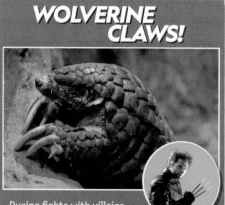

WOLVERINE

During fights with villains, Wolverine defends himself with long, sharp claws that pop out of his knuckles. Pangolins have claws on each of their front feet used to rip up ant and termite nests as they search for dinner. Claws also help them clutch onto branches or dig burrows for sleeping. Whether you're a superhero or a pangolin, claws really come in handy.

Eight species of pangolins exist in all.

The animal emits a stinky odor when threatened.

IRON-MAN ARMOR!

CLOSE-UP OF SCALES

IRON MAN

Iron Man sports a high-tech suit of armor that shields the superhero from weapons hurled by enemies. Pangolins wear armor, too. Their "suits" consist of rows of overlapping scales that resemble a pinecone. Made out of keratin—the same substance in your fingernails—the pangolin's armor is so tough that predators such as lions can't bite through it. It's too bad that this armor doesn't come with built-in jets!

ANT-MAN MOVES

ANT MAN

When he senses trouble, Ant-Man shrinks to the size of, well, an ant. Pangolins, which can be almost six feet (1.8 m) long from head to tail tip, have their own way of shrinking. If the mammal notices a nearby predator, it'll curl into a small ball less than half its normal size and shield its stomach and face. Unable to find a vulnerable part of the pangolin to strike, many enemies give up. Tiny can be tough.

TONGUE TIME

Up to 28 inches (71 cm) in all, a pangolin's tongue can be almost as long as its body (minus the tail)! How does it fit inside the mammal? The tongue runs from its mouth down its sternum (or breastbone). The back end curves around organs in the lower abdomen, arching toward the backbone. At rest, the tongue's front end is coiled inside the pangolin's mouth. The animal flicks out its licker to snag grub.

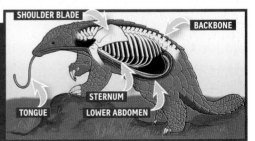

SHOULDER BLADE

BACKBONE

TONGUE

STERNUM

LOWER ABDOMEN

The Secret
Language
of
Dolphins

It's no secret that dolphins are able to chat with each other. Using squawks, clicks, and chirps, these smart animals communicate with distinctive dolphin chatter. But what are they saying? Scientists are trying to find out by studying wild and captive dolphins all over the world to decipher their secret language.

CHATTY Mammals

In many ways, you're just like the more than 30 species of dolphins that swim in the world's oceans and rivers. Dolphins are mammals, like you are, and must swim to the surface to breathe air. Just as you might, they team up in pods, or groups, to accomplish tasks. And they also talk to each other. "Sometimes one dolphin will vocalize and then another will seem to answer," says Sara Waller, who studies bottlenose dolphins off the California coast. "And sometimes members of a pod vocalize in different patterns at the same time, much like many people chattering at a party." And just as you gesture and change facial expressions as you talk, dolphins communicate nonverbally through body postures, jaw claps, bubble blowing, and fin caresses.

THINKING Dolphin

Scientists think dolphins "talk" about everything from basic facts like their age to their emotional state. "I speculate that they say things like 'Good fish are over here,' or 'Watch out for that shark because he's hunting,'" says Denise Herzing, who studies dolphins in the Bahamas. Sometimes, dolphins call for backup. After being bullied by a duo of bottlenose dolphins, one spotted dolphin returned to the scene the next day with a few pals to chase and harass one of the bully bottlenose dolphins. "It's as if the spotted dolphin communicated to his buddies that he needed their help, then led them in search of this guy," says Herzing, who watched the scuffle.

Want to have some fun?

Let's chase bubbles!

Back off, bud!

If you were a bottlenose dolphin, you could swim at a speed of 20 miles an hour (32 km/h). That's about four times as fast as an Olympic swimmer.

Toss me a treat!

Let's play!

5 to 20: individual dolphins in an average pod

Over 4: types of vocalizations dolphins use (These include squawks, whistles, clicks, and squeaks.)

12 miles (19 km): distance high-frequency whistles can travel

Over 30: nonverbal behaviors (for instance, tail slapping or rubbing fins) dolphins use to communicate

2 months: time before a baby dolphin is born that a mother might start "singing" to her unborn calf

LANGUAGE Lessons

Experts use high-tech gear to record and analyze every nuance of the dolphin language. But they're far from speaking "dolphin" yet. Part of the reason is because dolphins are hard to keep up with. Very fast swimmers, they stay underwater for up to 10 minutes between breaths. Also, their language is so dependent on what they're doing, whether they're playing, fighting, or going after tasty fish. It's no different for humans. Think about when you raise a hand to say hello. Under other circumstances, the same gesture can mean goodbye, stop, or that something costs five bucks. It's the same for dolphins. During fights, for example, dolphins clap their jaws to say "Back off!" But they jaw clap while playing too, as if to show who's king of the underwater playground. It's all a bit of a mystery.

So while scientists haven't completely cracked the code on dolphin chatter just yet, they're listening ... and learning.

I'm tougher than I look!

SEA OTTERS:
Super Cute, Super Tough

ULTIMATE FUR COAT

A sea otter wears a luxurious fur coat made up of about 800 million hairs. A shield from the sea, the coat is covered in natural oils that keep the skin and underfur dry. Because its fur is the only thing protecting a sea otter from the heat-stealing ocean water, the marine mammal spends nearly half of its day cleaning, combing, and fluffing its coat.

Only a female and her pups will hunt in groups or share food.

FEEDING FRENZY

To stay warm, an otter also relies on a super-revved metabolism. It must eat three times more calories than a kid needs in order to survive. A daily menu might be 7 abalone, 37 cancer crabs, 50 sea urchins, or 157 kelp crabs—that's about equal in calories to 42 scoops of chocolate ice cream! Otters also have to work for their food: To eat 150 kelp crabs, the otter needs to make at least 150 dives!

S ea otters may look like cute, gentle balls of fur, but they're actually rugged, resilient predators that battle prey, the environment, and other otters every day. Here's why they deserve a reputation as the tough guys of the ocean.

SEA SURVIVOR

A sea otter is about the same size as an 11-year-old kid—but a whole lot tougher. A human would be lucky to last 20 minutes in an otter's home just beyond the breaking waves before hypothermia— a drop in body temperature— set in and their body shut down. Unlike whales and walruses, otters don't even have blubber (a thick layer of fat) to keep them warm. So how do they survive?

Sea otters are related to skunks, weasels, badgers, and river otters.

SUPER STRENGTH

Sea otters are like superheroes when it comes to strength. A hard clam or mussel shell is no match for an otter's extremely powerful jaws and strong teeth. A person would have to use a special sharp tool to pry a firmly anchored abalone from its rock. An otter has only its paws and an occasional rock. The otter also uses its strong paws to snatch and overpower large crabs while avoiding their dangerous claws.

Super swimmers, super eaters, super divers— sea otters definitely deserve their rep as supertough marine mammals.

Incredible Powers
of the OCTOPUS!

POTIONS AND POISONS

Blue-ringed octopuses make one of the deadliest poisons in the world. They have enough poison in their saliva to kill a human, though these mollusks mostly use their venom to paralyze prey or to defend themselves from enemies.

TRICK ARMS

When faced with danger, some octopuses will break off an arm and scoot away. The arm keeps wriggling for hours, sometimes crawling all over an attacker and distracting it. The octopus grows a new arm out of the stump.

ESCAPE ARTIST

To confuse attackers, an octopus will squirt a concentrated ink out of its backside that forms a smokelike cloud. This allows enough time for an octopus to escape.

THE OCTOPUS IS THE TALLER LUMP ON THE RIGHT. THAT'S BRAIN CORAL ON THE LEFT.

MAGICAL MOVES

Octopuses can squeeze through tiny holes as if they were moving from room to room through keyholes. Some can even swim through the sand, sticking an eye up like a periscope to see if the coast is clear.

OCEAN SUPERSTARS

The fascinating lives of 6 sea turtle species

Think all sea turtles are the same? Think again! Each of these species stands out in its own way.

1 GREEN SEA TURTLE: THE NEAT FREAK

In Hawaii, U.S.A., green sea turtles choose a "cleaning station"—a location where groups of cleaner fish groom the turtles by eating ocean gunk, like algae and parasites, off their skin and shells. In Australia, the turtles rub against a favorite sponge or rock to scrub themselves. Neat!

2 KEMP'S RIDLEY: THE LITTLE ONE

They may be the smallest sea turtles (babies shown here), but they're not so tiny: Adults weigh as much as many 10-year-old kids, and their shell is about the size of a car tire. They're speedy, too: It takes them less than an hour to dig a nest, then lay and bury their eggs.

3 OLIVE RIDLEY: THE ULTRA-MOM

Every year, hundreds of thousands of female olive ridley sea turtles take over beaches to lay their eggs and then bury them before disappearing back into the sea. Call it safety in numbers: With thousands of turtles swarming the shoreline, they're sure to overwhelm any predator.

4 LEATHERBACK: THE MEGA-TURTLE

These giants among reptiles have shells about as big as a door and weigh as much as six professional football players! Their size doesn't slow them down, though. A leatherback can swim as fast as a bottlenose dolphin.

5 HAWKSBILL: THE HEARTY EATER

What's the hawksbill's favorite snack? Sponges! These turtles gobble about 1,200 pounds (544 kg) of sponges a year. The turtles can safely eat this sea life, which is toxic to other animals. That means there are plenty of sponges to snack on!

6 LOGGERHEAD: THE TOUGH GUY

The loggerhead sea turtle's powerful jaws can easily crack open the shells of lobsters, conchs, and snails to get at the meat inside. Some loggerheads swim a third of the way around the world to find food.

43

Animal

Red Fox

A newborn red fox hangs on a small shrub, likely accidentally dropped by his mother as she carried her litter to a new den. Without his mom to keep him warm on this winter night, he won't survive.

The next morning, a couple notices the kit. The woman scoops up the newborn in her hands, and feels him twitch. He's alive, but just barely.

OUT OF THE WOODS

The fox—now named Albert—is rushed to a wild animal veterinary hospital. Staff place Albert in a toasty incubator, and bottle-feed him formula. They also set a teddy bear beside him for snuggling. Within a few days, Albert perks up and scarfs down his meals.

FOX FRIENDS

When spring arrives about eight weeks later, Albert joins other rescued kits in a large enclosure next to the sanctuary. The little foxes chase and wrestle one another, practicing their stalking and pouncing skills—two abilities that will help them survive in the wild. Caregivers also hide dead squirrels and mice in their pen so the youngsters can practice hunting.

HOME STRETCH

Seven months after Albert's rescue, Albert and his fox pals are placed in a pen at the wooded release site, adapting to the sights, smells, and sounds of the wild. One night, Albert and the other foxes quietly slip back into the forest. They are back where they belong.

DINNER IS SERVED.

Bats

GETTING A BATH

FEEDING TIME

Rescues

Walking along the road at the foot of a hill in China's Sichuan Province, a group of people notice a giant panda on the hillside. Dazed, freezing, and starving, the panda has collapsed and is near death. The humans rush to alert officials—there is not much time left.

TO THE RESCUE
A rescuer shoots the panda with a tranquilizer dart, and the panda drifts off to sleep. They gently carry her down the hill and race her to a veterinary hospital. The underweight panda is infected with parasites and is suffering from hypothermia—when body temperature drops very low. With just some 1,800 giant pandas left in the wild, the caretakers know just how important it is to save this animal.

BAMBOO BONANZA
At first, the panda, Wolong II, just lies in her pen. But after a few days of rest and medicine, she sits up and begins munching on bamboo. The animal quickly gains more than 20 pounds (9 kg).

About six weeks after her rescue, Wolong II is healthy enough to return to the wild. She's secured in a metal crate and lifted into a truck. The rescue team carries the crate into the woods, and lays it down in a quiet spot surrounded by bamboo trees. They open its hatch, and Wolong II lumbers off into the forest without looking back.

Giant Panda

CARETAKERS AT THE HOSPITAL GIVE THE PANDA OXYGEN TO HELP HER BREATHE.

In eastern Australia, hundreds of baby bats were in trouble. The gray-headed flying foxes—who had not yet learned to fly—clung to their mothers, hanging high in a tree. But as a violent storm intensified, the wind knocked the babies from the shelter of their mothers' wings, and they fell to the ground. Wildlife volunteers rushed to the scene and discovered dozens of baby flying foxes lying helpless on the ground, 30 feet (9 m) below the tree.

The situation was scary, but after three long days, more than 350 little flying foxes were gently transported to a clinic. Bones were set, and antibiotics were given. Volunteers bottle-fed milk formula to the newborns every three hours. Soon, they graduated from bottles to solid foods, chowing down on chopped apples. They also learned to lap up nectar and finally figured out how to fly. After two and a half months at the clinic, the bats moved into an outside enclosure and eventually began to explore the wild, where they continued to thrive within the forest.

45

According to an ancient Native American legend, the Raven turned one out of every ten bears white to remind people of a time when Earth was covered by snow and ice.

Secrets
of the Spirit Bear

A rare animal creates a mysterious sight in the forest.

On a cold, rainy October night in the rain forest, a hulking white form with a ghostly glow appears in the distance. No, it's not the ghost of a black bear. It's a spirit bear, also called a Kermode bear, which is a black bear with white hair. Spirit bears live almost exclusively in one place: the Great Bear Rainforest along the coast of British Columbia, Canada. Researchers want to figure out why the bears with white coats have survived here. Fewer than 200 spirit bears call this area home.

WHITE COAT CLUES

For many animals, unusual white coloration can make it hard to survive because they may have trouble hiding from predators. But the Kermode bear's coloring may actually help it survive and give it an edge while catching salmon.

"A white bear blends into the background during the day and is more successful catching fish," explains biologist Thomas Reimchen. "There is an advantage to one bear in some conditions and the other in different conditions."

TALE OF TWO ISLANDS

Canada's Gribbell Island has the highest concentration of Kermode bears, followed by neighboring Princess Royal Island. These isolated islands may be another key to the bears' survival, since there's no competition from grizzly bears, and wolves are the only natural threat. The islands' trees provide shelters, and rivers are filled with salmon.

Even though spirit bears have flourished on these islands, new threats such as logging worry scientists and the members of the Native American Gitga'at First Nation, who have lived with and protected spirit bears for centuries. That's why researchers are working hard to understand the biology of the spirit bear. As they do, they can find the best ways to ensure its survival.

MONKEY TROUBLE
A YOUNG BABOON TAKES A DANGEROUS SWIM.

It's a chilly winter morning in Botswana's Okavango Delta in Africa. A troop of chacma baboons wades across a narrow stream. But an eight-month-old infant named Chobe is left behind. She frantically paces the shore and calls out. The others ignore her as they move through the cold water without her.

Because the baboons' territory is flooded for half of the year, they must cross water all day. They move from island to island to find food and to escape predators such as lions and leopards.

1 DANGEROUS CROSSING

To cross the stream, bigger kid baboons hitch a ride with one of their parents, climbing onto the adult's back. Chobe usually gets a lift across the water with her dad, but today he's gone on ahead. So she has to figure out a way to get across the water and keep up with her troop. A young baboon cannot survive alone in the wild.

2 CAUGHT IN THE CURRENT

Chobe begins to wade into the cold stream. The water quickly becomes too deep for her, so she starts to swim clumsily. Midway, the strong current drags her downstream, farther from the shore. Her screams turn to gurgles as she starts to swallow water.

3 COMFORT AFTER A CLOSE CALL

Chobe's tiring fast, but just then, her feet find a shallow bank in the stream and she races out of the water. She sits on the shore, shivering. Her mother soon arrives, holds her close, and grooms her. Grooming is a great form of comfort for baboons. In no time, Chobe is running around with the other young baboons.

4 STAYING SAFE WITH DAD

Baboons have to learn to survive on their own, and sometimes that involves dangerous lessons. Chobe got a taste of what it's like to be an independent member of the troop. She decides she isn't quite ready to be a grown-up yet ... so she makes sure to find her father and hop onto his back at the next water crossing.

BIZARRE Insects

Check out some of the strangest bugs on Earth!

The bright-colored head of the puss moth caterpillar warns predators to stay away. This species, one of the most toxic caterpillars in North America, can spray acid from its head when it is attacked.

puss moth caterpillar

walking leaf

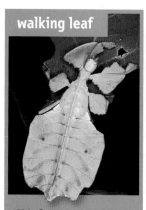

This flat, green insect is a master of disguise: It's common to mistake this bug for an actual leaf, thanks to its large, feathery wings. This clever camouflage provides protection from potential predators.

giraffe-necked weevil

No surprise, this bug gets its name from its extra-long neck. The males have longer necks than females do, which they use to fight other males for mating rights.

thorn bugs

One tiny thorn bug may not be a match for a bigger predator, but when grouped together on a branch, these spiky bugs create a prickly pack no bird wants a bite of!

spiny katydid

This katydid is covered in sharper-than-knives spikes. If a predator attacks, this species springs into action, defending itself by jabbing an enemy with its spiny legs and arms.

cockchafer beetle

The wild, feathery antennae on the male cockchafer may be cool to look at, but they're also helpful tools. They enable the bug to sniff for food and feel out its surrounding environment.

acorn weevil

The acorn weevil's hollow nose is longer than its body, and perfect for drilling through the shells of acorns. A female will feast on the nut by sucking up its rich, fatty liquid, and then lay her eggs in the acorn.

pink grasshopper

Though most grasshoppers are green or brown, some—like this pink nymph—are much brighter. Pink grasshoppers are rare, most likely because they are easy for predators to spot.

man-faced stinkbug

There are more than 4,500 species of stinkbugs worldwide, including this brilliant yellow species, whose shield-shaped body displays a unique pattern resembling a tribal mask. Like all stinkbugs, this species secretes a foul-smelling liquid from scent glands between its legs when it feels threatened.

rhinoceros beetle

Ounce for ounce, this insect, which gets its name from the hornlike structure on the male's head, is considered one of the world's strongest creatures. It is capable of carrying up to 850 times its own body weight.

5 COOL THINGS ABOUT Butterflies

MONARCH PUPA

2 Butterflies are nature's magicians.

Butterflies begin life as caterpillars. Once grown, the caterpillar becomes a pupa. Protected by a cocoon, the pupa transforms into a butterfly, a process called metamorphosis.

1 Some butterflies start out smelly.

Not all butterflies stink, but the caterpillar of the zebra swallowtail butterfly sure does! Its nasty odor helps keep it safe from hungry animals.

ZEBRA SWALLOWTAIL

3 Butterflies taste WITH THEIR "FEET."

Butterflies have chemical receptors on their legs, similar to taste buds, that allow them to taste the sweetness of a peach just by standing on it.

4 MANY butterflies ARE poisonous.

The monarch, for example, eats only poisonous milkweed plants, making both the caterpillar and the adult butterfly a dangerous snack for predators.

5 Some are winged tricksters.

Owl butterflies startle predators with huge "eyes" on their wings. The false eyes divert an attacker's attention, giving the butterfly time for a hasty escape.

OWL BUTTERFLY

Bet You Didn't Know

8 surprising facts about spiders

1 Golden silk orb-weaver spiders vibrate their webs to distract predators.

2 Black widow spiders are more **venomous** than rattlesnakes.

3 After a large meal, a tarantula may not **eat** for a month.

4 Crab spiders **change color** to blend in with their surroundings.

5 There are more than 37,000 species of spiders.

6 A spider **eats** about **2,000 insects** a year.

7 The **oldest** known spider fossils are more than **300 million** years old.

8 A pound (.45 kg) of **spider silk** could stretch around the Equator.

Does Your Pet L♥ve You?

More scientists are beginning to agree with what most pet owners already believe: Pets do love the people in their lives. Decide for yourself!

Rescue Dog ♡

When two-year-old Daisy Smith wandered from her family's yard one day, she was lucky to have her family's Labrador retriever, Thunder, tagging along. After 13 hours, a search party finally found the little girl (right) sitting by a river a mile and a half (2.4 km) from her home, with Thunder by her side. There's no doubt that this hero dog loves his Daisy!

Fire Cat

Boo Boo the cat is living proof that animals are capable of unselfish love. One night, as Frances Morris and her husband were asleep in their bed, Boo Boo began meowing and howling. Sleepily, Morris tried to calm Boo Boo, but the cat kept meowing. Fully awake, Morris realized the bedroom was filling with smoke. The kitchen was on fire! Instead of escaping outside, Boo Boo had run upstairs to warn the Morrises, and everyone escaped safely.

Funny Bunny

Who needs jokes when you have a bunny? That's what 13-year-old Kenny Clessas discovered when his pet rabbit, Killer, got him giggling after a bad day. Noticing Kenny crying, Killer started head-butting and running circles around the boy. Kenny just had to laugh!

How affectionate is your pet?

1

When you arrive at home, your dog ...

a. hides under the couch.

b. barely looks up from its nap.

c. runs to greet you.

2

Whenever you sit down on a chair or the floor, your cat ...

a. leaves the room.

b. watches you from afar.

c. cuddles up on your lap, purring.

3

If you reach into the cage, your gerbil ...

a. digs into its wood chips to hide.

b. backs away unless coaxed with a treat.

c. jumps onto your hand eagerly.

IF YOUR ANSWER IS a, your pet plays it cool. It decides when it's cuddle time. b, your pet thinks you're its buddy. It likes you to be around. c, your pet is head over heels in love with you. It would do anything to be close to you.

A PUZZLE FOR YOUR POOCH

DISCOVER HOW FAST YOUR DOG LEARNS

Your new puppy wants a bit of your pizza. He tries sitting at your feet and whining. No deal. He paws at your knee and gets pushed away. Then he notices that your baby sister dropped some on the floor. Score! Tomorrow night, he'll head straight for the baby's chair. That's learning. You can test your dog's ability to learn by giving him this puzzle and seeing if he can solve it faster with practice.

YOU NEED

9 bite-size treats

3 tennis balls

muffin tin

stopwatch or clock

pencil and paper

INSTRUCTIONS

1 Set three treats into different holes in the muffin tin. Show the muffin tin to your dog to get him interested.

2 Place a tennis ball on top of each treat and set the muffin tin on the floor.

3 Start timing. Record how long it takes your dog to uncover all three treats.

4 Repeat the procedure and record how long it takes him to find all the treats a second time.

5 Give him one more round and record the time for his third attempt.

6 Compare the three times. If your dog was faster on his second and third tries, it shows that he learned how to extract the treats quickly.

Whenever a dog does something and gets a reward, he is more likely to do it again. Psychologists call this conditioning. The problem is, dogs are in constant motion. It takes a lot of work to teach them which move is being rewarded. You can almost imagine your dog's thoughts the first time you reward him for a trick, "Oh, I wagged my tail. Is that why I got the treat? I sneezed. Did that do it? Maybe she gave me a treat because I wiggled my ears." Gradually, your dog will realize which action earns the treat.

Treat puzzles work similarly. Spot smells the treat and knows it's there. He may try several ways to get it out: nudging with his nose, pushing with his paw, and looking at you to see if you'll get it for him. With enough practice, he'll figure out the best way to get the treat, and soon he'll be gulping them down.

TIP

If the ball sinks all the way into the muffin tin opening, it may be difficult for your dog to move the ball. Try using a muffin tin with slightly narrower openings or a thick treat that will elevate the ball a little.

Check out the book!

20 CUTEST ANIMALS OF 2020

From furry bobcats to smiling geckos, there's no shortage of cute creatures on Earth. Here's NG Kids' roundup of cuddly critters that are sure to make you say *awww.*

1 GET UP, STAND UP

A group of meerkats stands at attention by its burrow. Extremely family-oriented, meerkat "mobs" spend a lot of time playing together in a tight-knit group. The furry family may look sweet, but if confronted, they will stand together, arching their backs, raising their hair, and hissing.

2 CLOSE-UP

This young wombat is definitely not camera shy! Native to Australia, these marsupials are about the size of a jelly bean at birth and stay in their mom's pouch for several months before venturing out, where they'll spend most of their days burrowing underground tunnels.

3 TRUNK SHOW

Get out of these elephants' way! African elephants can weigh some 200 pounds (91 kg) at birth; by adulthood, they can top the scales at more than seven tons (6.4 t). The world's largest land mammal also has a big appetite, eating more than 300 pounds (136 kg) of grass, fruit, and leaves a day.

5 THINK PINK

Adult greater flamingos may be famous for their coral-colored hue, but their chicks look a lot different—at first. Born with gray or white feathers, it takes two to three years for a young flamingo's pink feathers to show.

4 SPOT ON

This cuddly-looking bobcat may have one of the finest fur coats in the animal world, but it's not all about looking good. The spotted fur helps North America's most common wild cat blend in with many habitats. Those ear tufts? Bobcats may twitch them to communicate with other bobcats.

6

BEAR-Y HUNGRY

In the fall, this brown bear cub will start packing on about three pounds (1.4 kg) a day to prepare for its deep winter sleep. Those pounds of fat are what the bear will live on while snoozing. Luckily, Mom is an expert at sniffing out a meal in their northwestern U.S. habitat and can detect food from 18 miles (29 km) away.

7

HANGING OUT

This young raccoon might be an expert climber—many raccoons spend their first few months living in a nest in a tree hole. As adults, raccoons rely more on their sense of touch than on their senses of sight and smell to find meals such as frogs, bird eggs, insects, and even snakes.

8

UP A TREE

This baby orangutan may have figured out the best part of life in the trees: just hanging out! Orangutans spend up to 95 percent of their time high up in trees on the Southeast Asia islands of Borneo and Sumatra. They sleep, eat, and play in nests that are big enough for a 10-year-old kid to stretch out in.

9 RAD REPTILE

The gentle leopard gecko is famous for its spots as well as for its urine, which comes out as tiny crystals. Its calm nature and long life span—it can live up to 20 years if treated well—make this gecko a very popular pet.

ALL EARS

Nobody sports a birthday suit better than a baby aardvark. Born pink and wrinkly, this big baby slurps milk but will gobble thousands of ants a night when it's older. An African native, the aardvark's name means "earth pig" in one South African language. It has donkey ears, a kangaroo tail, and a piggy nose, but it's actually a distant relation to the elephant.

10

11

FLYING LEAP

Caracals may not have wings, but they can sure fly! This small wild cat, native to Africa and the Middle East, has strong hind legs that allow it to jump more than six feet (2 m) in the air—the height of a tall adult human.

12

HANGING ON

This 10-month-old gorilla keeps a tight hold on a bamboo pole in Volcanoes National Park in Rwanda, Africa. Gorillas are born with a powerful grip, which allows them to hang on to their moms for transport—and, of course, to climb.

BLENDING IN

Hares, beware! This critter may look adorable, but it could be your enemy. Silent and sneaky, the ermine can pounce on prey that's larger than it is, such as an arctic hare. The stealthy stalker gets help from its changing coat, which is white during winter and brown in spring and summer—perfect camouflage.

13

14

STARTING SMALL

Coyote pups may be tiny at first, but they eventually grow to be the size of medium dogs. They're cared for from birth by both parents, who give their offspring an early start on hunting by bringing live mice to their den for stalking practice.

WHAT A HOOT!

Why, hello there! A Eurasian pygmy owl peers out of a tree in a forest in Sweden. These tiny owls—which grow to be about the size of a robin—are small enough to squeeze into tree holes made by woodpeckers, where they build their nests.

15

SMILEY SQUID

Say cheese? It may look like this piglet squid is smiling, but in reality this deepwater dweller isn't quite hamming for the camera. Rather, the squid's friendly "face" is the result of tentacles and unusual skin patterns, which form the shape of an adorable mug topped by a mop of curly hair.

16

18

TALL TALE

Talk about a grand entrance: A baby giraffe falls about six feet (1.8 m) from its mom during birth before hitting the ground. But the bumpy landing doesn't stop the little guys from getting a jump start on life—they're usually up on their hooves and walking at just an hour old.

17

JUST LION AROUND

A mother Galápagos sea lion lounges around with her pup. These animals share a tight bond: Although baby sea lions usually learn to swim by the time they're two weeks old, they stick to their mothers' sides for a few years before venturing out on their own.

BADGE OF HONOR

What's black and white and striped all over? An American badger, of course! This species is easily recognized by the telltale white stripe, which runs from the tip of their noses all the way to the back of their heads. But it's the badgers' black cheek patches—called "badges"— that give them their name.

19

HOP TO IT

Native to tropical Amazon forests, this frog's see-through skin helps it hide high in the trees. Sunlight shines right through the frog and provides camouflage. When it's time to lay its eggs, a glass frog deposits tiny white eggs onto a leaf above a stream. When the tadpoles emerge, they slip off the leaf and splash into the water below.

20

63

Prehistoric TIMELINE

HUMANS HAVE WALKED on Earth for some 200,000 years, a mere blip in the planet's 4.5-billion-year history. A lot has happened during that time. Earth formed, and oxygen levels rose in the millions of years of the Precambrian time. The productive Paleozoic era gave rise to hard-shelled organisms, vertebrates, amphibians, and reptiles.

Dinosaurs ruled Earth in the mighty Mesozoic. And 65 million years after dinosaurs became extinct, modern humans emerged in the Cenozoic era. From the first tiny mollusks to the dinosaur giants of the Jurassic and beyond, Earth has seen a lot of transformation.

THE PRECAMBRIAN TIME

4.5 billion to 542 million years ago

- Earth (and other planets) formed from gas and dust left over from a giant cloud that collapsed to form the sun. The giant cloud's collapse was triggered when nearby stars exploded.
- Low levels of oxygen made Earth a suffocating place.
- Early life-forms appeared.

THE PALEOZOIC ERA

542 million to 252 million years ago

- The first insects and other animals appeared on land.
- 450 million years ago (m.y.a.), the ancestors of sharks began to swim in the oceans.
- 430 m.y.a., plants began to take root on land.
- More than 360 m.y.a., amphibians emerged from the water.
- Slowly, the major landmasses began to come together, creating Pangaea, a single supercontinent.
- By 300 m.y.a., reptiles had begun to dominate the land.

What Killed the Dinosaurs?

It's a mystery that's boggled the minds of scientists for centuries: What happened to the dinosaurs? While various theories have bounced around, a recent study confirms that the most likely culprit is an asteroid or comet that created a giant crater. Researchers say that the impact set off a series of natural disasters like tsunamis, earthquakes, and temperature swings that plagued the dinosaurs' ecosystem and disrupted their food chain. This, paired with intense volcanic eruptions that caused drastic climate changes, is thought to be why half of the world's species—including the dinosaurs—died in a mass extinction.

THE MESOZOIC ERA

251 million to 65 million years ago

The Mesozoic era, or the age of the reptiles, consisted of three consecutive time periods (shown below). This is when the first dinosaurs began to appear. They would reign supreme for more than 150 million years.

TRIASSIC PERIOD

251 million to 201 million years ago

- Appearance of the first mammals. They were rodent-size.
- The first dinosaur appeared.
- Ferns were the dominant plants on land.
- The giant supercontinent of Pangaea began breaking up toward the end of the Triassic.

JURASSIC PERIOD

201 million to 145 million years ago

- Giant dinosaurs dominated the land.
- Pangaea continued its breakup, and oceans formed in the spaces between the drifting landmasses, allowing sea life, including sharks and marine crocodiles, to thrive.
- Conifer trees spread across the land.

CRETACEOUS PERIOD

145 million to 66 million years ago

- The modern continents developed.
- The largest dinosaurs developed.
- Flowering plants spread across the landscape.
- Mammals flourished, and giant pterosaurs ruled the skies over small birds.
- Temperatures grew more extreme. Dinosaurs lived in deserts, swamps, and forests from the Antarctic to the Arctic.

THE CENOZOIC ERA—TERTIARY PERIOD

65 million to 2.6 million years ago

- Following the dinosaur extinction, mammals rose as the dominant species.
- Birds continued to flourish.
- Volcanic activity was widespread.
- Temperatures began to cool, eventually ending in an ice age.
- The period ended with land bridges forming, which allowed plants and animals to spread to new areas.

DINO TIMES

DINO Classification

Classifying dinosaurs and all other living things can be a complicated matter, so scientists have devised a system to help with the process. Dinosaurs are put into groups based on a very large range of characteristics.

Scientists put dinosaurs into two major groups: the bird-hipped ornithischians and the lizard-hipped saurischians.

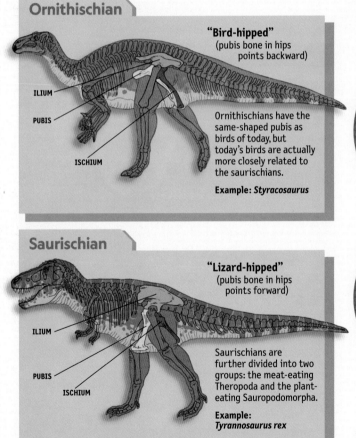

Ornithischian

ILIUM

PUBIS

ISCHIUM

"Bird-hipped"
(pubis bone in hips points backward)

Ornithischians have the same-shaped pubis as birds of today, but today's birds are actually more closely related to the saurischians.

Example: *Styracosaurus*

Saurischian

ILIUM

PUBIS

ISCHIUM

"Lizard-hipped"
(pubis bone in hips points forward)

Saurischians are further divided into two groups: the meat-eating Theropoda and the plant-eating Sauropodomorpha.

Example: *Tyrannosaurus rex*

Within these two main divisions, dinosaurs are then separated into orders and then families, such as Stegosauria. Like other members of the Stegosauria, *Stegosaurus* had spines and plates along the back, neck, and tail.

THE FIERCE ALLOSAURUS HAD NEARLY **70** TEETH.

CORYTHOSAURUS LIVED IN BIG HERDS LIKE MODERN BUFFALO.

BRACHIOSAURUS WAS TALLER THAN **TWO** GIRAFFES.

THE *SPINOSAURUS* ATE SHARKS.

③ NEWLY DISCOVERED DINOS

Humans have been searching for—and discovering—dinosaur remains for hundreds of years. In that time, at least 1,000 species of dinos have been found all over the world, and thousands more may still be out there waiting to be unearthed. Recent discoveries include *Borealopelta markmitchelli*. Found in western Canada, the plant-eating armored dinosaur is so well preserved that paleontologists have discovered remnants of its skin.

① *Borealopelta markmitchelli* (Ornithischian)

Named After: Mark Mitchell, the man who chipped the rock away from the fossil

Length: 18 feet (5.5 m)

Time Range: Cretaceous

Where: Alberta, Canada

② *Mansourasaurus shahinae* (Saurischian)

Named After: Mansoura University in Egypt

Length: 33 feet (10 m)

Time Range: Late Cretaceous

Where: Egypt

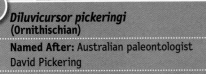

③ *Diluvicursor pickeringi* (Ornithischian)

Named After: Australian paleontologist David Pickering

Length: 7.5 feet (2.3 m)

Time Range: Cretaceous

Where: Australian-Antarctic rift valley

DINO DEFENSES

Scientists don't know for sure whether plant-eating dinos used their amazing attributes to battle their carnivorous cousins, but these herbivores were armed with some pretty wicked ways they could have used to defend themselves.

ARMOR: *GASTONIA*
(GAS-TONE-EE-AH)

Prickly *Gastonia* was covered in heavy, defensive armor. To protect it from the strong jaws of meat-eaters it had four horns on its head, thick layers of bone shielding its brain, rows of spikes sticking out from its back, and a tail with triangular blades running along each side.

SPIKES: *KENTROSAURUS*
(KEN-TROH-SORE-US)

Stand back! This cousin of *Stegosaurus* had paired spikes along its tail, which it could swing at attackers with great speed. One paleontologist estimated that *Kentrosaurus* could have swung its treacherous tail fast enough to shatter bones!

CLUB TAILZ:
ANKYLOSAURUS
(AN-KYE-LOH-SORE-US)

Steer clear! *Ankylosaurus* possessed a heavy, knobby tail that it could have used to whack attackers. It may not have totally protected the tanklike late Cretaceous dino from a determined *T. rex*, but a serious swing could have generated enough force to do some real damage to its rival reptile.

WHIP TAIL:
DIPLODOCUS
(DIH-PLOD-UH-KUS)

Some scientists think this late Jurassic giant's tail—about half the length of its 90-foot (27-m) body—could have been used like a whip and swished at high speeds, creating a loud noise that would send potential predators running.

HORNS:
TRICERATOPS
(TRI-SER-UH-TOPS)

There's no evidence *Triceratops* ever used its horns to combat late Cretaceous snack-craving carnivores. But scientists do believe the famous three-horned creature used its frills and horns in battle with other members of its species.

Dynamite
DINO AWARDS

Spiky body armor. Razor-sharp teeth. Unimaginable strength. No doubt, all dinos are cool. But whether they were the biggest, the fiercest, or the biggest-brained of the bunch, some stand out more than others. Here are seven of the most amazing dinos ever discovered.

Supersize Appetite

Big Brain

Scientists think that *Tyrannosaurus rex* could gulp down 500 pounds (227 kg) of meat at a time—that's like eating 2,000 hamburger patties in one bite!

Troodon, a meat-eater the size of a man, had a brain as big as an avocado pit—relatively large for a dinosaur of its small stature. Because of its big brain, scientists think *Troodon* may have been the smartest dino and as intelligent as modern birds.

Cool Camo

The birdlike *Sinornithosaurus* had feathers similar to those of modern birds. It may have also had reddish brown, yellow, and black coloring that kept this turkey-size raptor camouflaged as it hunted in the forest.

Heavy-weight

The heaviest of all dinosaurs, *Argentinosaurus* is believed to have weighed 220,000 pounds (99,790 kg)—more than 15 elephants.

Pint-Size Predator

Microraptor zhaoianus, the smallest meat-eating dinosaur, measured just 16 inches (40 cm) tall. With long toe tips for grasping branches, it's thought to be closely related to today's birds.

Built for Speed

Ornithomimids, a group of dinosaurs that resembled ostriches, would have given the world's fastest man a run for his money. Some of these long-limbed, toothless meat-eaters are thought to have clocked speeds of 50 miles an hour (80 km/h).

Super Spines

Known as the "spine lizard," *Spinosaurus* had huge spines sticking out of its back, some taller than a fourth grader! Weighing up to 22 tons (20 t), it may have been the biggest meat-eating dinosaur.

QUIZ WHIZ

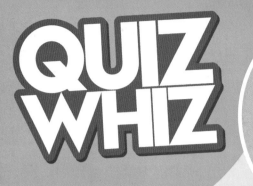

Explore just how much you know about animals with this quiz!
Write your answers on a piece of paper. Then check them below.

1. **Sea otters are related to _____.**
   a. skunks
   b. dolphins
   c. sloths
   d. narwhals

2. **One of the red-eyed tree frog's calls sounds like a _____.**
   a. car horn
   b. baby rattle
   c. guitar
   d. cricket

3. **True or false?** A margay's ankle can rotate all the way around to face backward.

4. **Which dinosaur feature is believed to have been used for defense?**
   a. knobby tail
   b. horns and frills
   c. thick layer of bone
   d. all of the above

5. **Which is not a characteristic of birds?**
   a. They lay eggs.
   b. They breathe with lungs.
   c. They are cold-blooded.
   d. They have feathers and wings.

Not **STUMPED** yet? Check out the *NATIONAL GEOGRAPHIC KIDS QUIZ WHIZ* collection for more crazy **ANIMAL** questions!

ANSWERS: 1. a; 2. b; 3. True; 4. d; 5. c

72

HOMEWORK HELP

Wildly Good Animal Reports

Seahorse

Your teacher wants a written report on the seahorse. Not to worry. Use these organizational tools so you can stay afloat while writing a report.

STEPS TO SUCCESS: Your report will follow the format of a descriptive or expository essay (see p. 199 for "How to Write a Perfect Essay") and should consist of a main idea, followed by supporting details and a conclusion. Use this basic structure for each paragraph as well as the whole report, and you'll be on the right track.

1. Introduction

State your **main idea.**

Seahorses are fascinating fishes with many unique characteristics.

2. Body

Provide **supporting points** for your main idea.

Seahorses are very small fishes.

Seahorses are named for their head shape.

Seahorses display behavior that is rare among almost all other animals on Earth.

Then **expand** on those points with further description, explanation, or discussion.

Seahorses are very small fishes.

Seahorses are about the size of an M&M at birth, and most adult seahorses would fit in a teacup.

Seahorses are named for their head shape.

With long, tubelike snouts, seahorses are named for their resemblance to horses. A group of seahorses is called a herd.

Seahorses display behavior that is rare among almost all other animals on Earth.

Unlike most other fish, seahorses stay with one mate their entire lives. They are also among the only species in which dads, not moms, give birth to the babies.

3. Conclusion

Wrap it up with a **summary** of your whole paper.

Because of their unique shape and unusual behavior, seahorses are among the most fascinating and easily distinguishable animals in the ocean.

KEY INFORMATION

Here are some things you should consider including in your report:

What does your animal look like?
To what other species is it related?
How does it move?
Where does it live?
What does it eat?
What are its predators?
How long does it live?
Is it endangered?
Why do you find it interesting?

SEPARATE FACT FROM FICTION: Your animal may have been featured in a movie or in myths and legends. Compare and contrast how the animal has been portrayed with how it behaves in reality. For example, penguins can't dance the way they do in *Happy Feet.*

PROOFREAD AND REVISE: As with any great essay, when you're finished, check for misspellings, grammatical mistakes, and punctuation errors. It often helps to have someone else proofread your work, too, as he or she may catch things you have missed. Also, look for ways to make your sentences and paragraphs even better. Add more descriptive language, choosing just the right verbs, adverbs, and adjectives to make your writing come alive.

BE CREATIVE: Use visual aids to make your report come to life. Include an animal photo file with interesting images found in magazines or printed from websites. Or draw your own! You can also build a miniature animal habitat diorama. Use creativity to help communicate your passion for the subject.

THE FINAL RESULT: Put it all together in one final, polished draft. Make it neat and clean, and remember to cite your references.

SCIENCE and TECHNOLOGY

It's a bird, it's a plane, it's a ... driverless air taxi? Volocopter 2X, still in the prototype stage, can transport two passengers. The 18-rotor drone aircraft is being tested in Dubai.

EARTH EXPLORER
Meet Kakani Katija!

This National Geographic emerging explorer blends biology and math to create cool tools.

Kakani Katija loved science and math growing up, so she thought she would be an astronaut one day. But after discovering she had a passion for bioengineering—the combination of engineering and biology—she decided to dive into an even deeper area: the ocean.

Today, Kakani develops instruments to enable exploration of previously hard-to-reach areas, like far below the ocean's surface. At the Monterey Bay Aquarium Research Institute (MBARI), Kakani created a tool called DeepPIV (short for Particle Image Velocimetry) that measures tiny plastic particles called microplastics thousands of meters underwater—and the animals that eat them.

"The tool uses laser illumination to see how these animals consume plastics," she says of DeepPIV, which is attached to a submersible robot that can travel 2.5 miles

(4,000 m) below the ocean's surface. "Many people assume that the plastic problem is constrained to the surface of the ocean. What we discovered is that there are microplastics in the deepest parts, even on the ocean floor, and there are animals ingesting them."

By continuing to develop better observational tools and techniques, Kakani can arm biologists and other experts with more knowledge about what's going on in the deep sea. She hopes this will trigger change that can ultimately improve the condition of our oceans—and the entire planet.

"It's hard to come up with the best solutions if you don't know what the problem is," says Kakani. "As bioengineers, we use technology to find new ways to approach a problem, and help others fix it."

8 million tons (7.2 million t) of trash wind up in the ocean each year.

MICROPLASTICS

> " I was always enamored by the search for life in outer planets. And then I realized that there is a lot of life in our oceans that we knew almost nothing about. That story is just beginning. "

KAKANI OPERATING DEEPPIV

It took about four years for Kakani and her team to design, build, and finally use the DeepPIV tool.

CALL TO ACTION!

Want to get into bioengineering? Better start crunching some numbers. "Math is the foundation of any bio-engineering career," says Kakani. "Our focus is on finding solutions." To do your part in reducing the amount of plastics that DeepPIV finds in the ocean, a good place to start is by using reusable straws instead of plastic ones. Encourage your friends and family to do the same!

INSPECTING A FISHING NET FOUND IN THE OCEAN

COOL INVENTIONS

FLOATING ISLAND

You'd *want* to be stranded on this island. Modeled after a large species of lily pad that drifts down the Amazon River, the Lilypad floating ecopolis is designed to float on the ocean. This human-made habitat would feature homes and shops structured around a lagoon that could collect rain for drinking water. Fueled in part by wind and solar power, the island concept could provide up to 50,000 residents with an eco-friendly home—and the ultimate oceanfront view.

PART OF THE ISLAND HABITAT DIPS UNDERWATER.

GLOVES GIVE CONCERT

These gloves hit the right notes. Sensors inside the fingertips detect when you press on a hard surface and send a signal to a speaker to produce the same musical notes created by hitting piano keys. Tap out a tune with your hands side by side. Then move your mitts away from each other and drum your fingers again. The sensors can tell that your digits have moved, and they signal the speaker to play different notes—same as if you moved your hands in different directions on an actual piano. That rocks!

TAP YOUR FINGERS!

ROBOT FOLDS LAUNDRY

Doing laundry is no longer such a chore with FoldiMate, a robot that folds clean clothes. All you have to do is clip garments to hangers on the machine's exterior. The hangers, attached to a conveyor belt, rotate downward, pulling articles of clothing one at a time into a slot. Inside the robot, an electronic arm plucks each garment from its hanger and lays it on a platform. Here, more arms fold and dispense the item. Soon your laundry's done—case *clothed*.

BEFORE

AFTER

BATTER GOES HERE.

THE MACHINE MADE THESE PANCAKES!

PANCAKE ART

Create art with pancake mix! The PancakeBot produces flapjacks shaped as the Eiffel Tower, George Washington, Scooby-Doo, and more. First, use the PancakeBot computer program to trace over a design with the drawing tool. The movements are translated into step-by-step instructions for the PancakeBot to follow. Now just pour batter into the machine. The bot's electronic nozzle will squeeze the mixture onto a heated griddle below, shifting as it follows the directions to create the flapjack formation. The result? Pancakes that look *almost* too good to eat.

RAIN ALERT!

9:41

UMBRELLA PREDICTS WEATHER

Getting caught in the rain is no fun. That's where the Oombrella comes in. This umbrella's handle contains a device that measures temperature, air pressure, and humidity to predict exactly when it's going to rain. Connecting wirelessly to your phone, it alerts you about 15 minutes before the first drops fall. And don't worry about accidentally leaving this gear at a friend's house once the skies clear. The Oombrella pings your phone if you're more than 130 feet (40 m) away from it. That's one unforgettable umbrella.

SPACE GLIDER

The Perlan 2 plane will sweep you 17 miles (27 km) off the ground to the edge of space—and it doesn't even have an engine, jets, or propellers. What the two-passenger glider *does* have is an 84-foot (26-m) wingspan, about the length of two school buses. To take off, this lightweight craft is connected by cable to another plane and towed 10,000 feet (3,050 m) into the air. Then it's released over mountainous regions where extra-strong air currents buoy the plane under its large wings and carry the craft 90,000 feet (27,500 m) high. Here, data is collected on the atmosphere before pilots use the glider's air brakes to descend. Glide on!

PILOT

AIRBUS

FUTURE WORLD:

The year is 2070 and it's time to get dressed for school. You step in front of a large video mirror that projects different clothes on you. After you decide on your favorite T-shirt, a robot fetches your outfit. No time is lost trying to find matching socks! Chores? What chores? Get ready for a whole new home life.

STAY CONNECTED

Whether your future home is an urban skyscraper or an underwater pod, all buildings will one day be connected via a central communications hub. Want to check out a *T. rex* skeleton at a faraway museum? You can virtually connect to it just as though you were checking it out in person. But you're not just seeing something miles away. Connect to a beach house's balcony and smell the salt water and feel the breeze. Buildings might also share information about incoming weather and emergencies to keep you safe.

CUSTOM COMFORT

Soon, your house may give you a personal welcome home. No need for keys—sensors scan your body and open the door. Walk into the living room, and the lighting adjusts to your preferred setting. Thirsty? A glass of water pops up on the counter. Before bed, you enter the bathroom and say, "Shower, please." The water starts flowing at exactly the temperature you want.

ON LOCATION

Your room has a spectacular view of the ocean ... because your house is suspended above it. New technologies will allow us to build our homes in unusual spots. In the future, "floating" structures elevated by supporting poles above water or other hard-to-access spots (think mountain peaks) will be more common as cities become more crowded. And this won't be limited to dry land on Earth. That means one day, your family could even live in space!

Homes

ON THE GO

Homes of the future will always be on the move. Walls will be capable of expanding and contracting, and houses will rotate with the sun's movements to conserve energy. Buildings will also be capable of changing size depending on who's inside. Grandparents could "move in" by attaching a modular section to the front, back, or top of the house.

BRING ON THE BOTS

While you were outside playing with your friends, your house robot did the laundry, vacuumed, and cleaned the bathroom. Meanwhile a drone just delivered groceries for the home-bot to put away. Minutes later, lunch is ready. The service is great ... but how will you earn your allowance? Instead of taking out the garbage or setting the table, you'll earn money by helping clean and maintain the robots.

FUTURE WORLD:

How do you get to the store in the year 2060? It's raining, so you decide not to take the drone. Instead you ride in your driverless cube car.

"The sky's no longer the limit in terms of where transportation is headed," says Tom Kurfess, a mechanical engineering professor at the Georgia Institute of Technology. Take a peek at these wild rides of the future.

GOING UP ... WAY UP!

The space elevator doors open—welcome to the space station lobby. It's possible that people will one day ride a space elevator from Earth to a space station that orbits our planet from 22,370 miles (36,000 km) above. The elevator will carry passengers and cargo into space without burning huge amounts of fuel, unlike today's rockets. Aboard the station, travelers might stay in a hotel room with a truly out-of-this-world view. Then those heading to, say, Mars, can transfer to a spaceship to continue their journey.

NO DRIVER NEEDED

You exit your high-rise apartment balcony into your own private glass elevator, take a seat, and say your destination. The elevator car descends 205 floors to street level before detaching from the building and moving to the street. It's now a cube-shaped car. Another cube carrying your friends is nearby; the vehicles connect while in motion, transforming into one bigger car. The cube drops you off at school and parks itself. According to Tommaso Gecchelin, founder of NEXT Future Transportation, driverless cars will work together to end traffic jams and improve safety.

Transportation

POWER PLANE

Passenger planes will still be around in the future—they'll just travel *much* faster. Today flying 6,850 miles (11,025 km) from New York City to Beijing, China, takes about 14 hours. But thanks to future technological advancements such as sleeker, more lightweight aircraft, a passenger plane could make the same trip in just under two hours.

FLOWN BY DRONE

"One day soon drones and robots will deliver our meals," Gecchelin says. But further into the future, helicopter-size drones could also deliver *people*. Some experts even think that cargo drones will be able to lift small houses from a city and carry them to scenic vacation spots.

TOTALLY TUBULAR

Your friend invites you to her birthday party. It's today—and across the country. No prob. You can tube it from the West Coast to the East Coast in just two hours. You sit in a capsule that looks like a train without rails. *Whoosh!* The capsule's sucked into a vacuum tube. Like a bullet train, the capsule uses magnets to fly forward in the tube without friction or resistance. The result: a smooth, fast ride that never slows down below 750 miles an hour (1,200 km/h).

WHAT IS LIFE?

This seems like such an easy question to answer. Everybody knows that singing birds are alive and rocks are not. But when we start studying bacteria and other microscopic creatures, things get more complicated.

SO WHAT EXACTLY IS LIFE?

Most scientists agree that something is alive if it can do the following: reproduce; grow in size to become more complex in structure; take in nutrients to survive; give off waste products; and respond to external stimuli, such as increased sunlight or changes in temperature.

KINDS OF LIFE

Biologists classify living organisms by how they get their energy. Organisms such as algae, green plants, and some bacteria use sunlight as an energy source. Animals (like humans), fungi, and some Archaea use chemicals to provide energy. When we eat food, chemical reactions within our digestive system turn our food into fuel.

Living things inhabit land, sea, and air. In fact, life also thrives deep beneath the oceans, embedded in rocks miles below Earth's crust, in ice, and in other extreme environments. The life-forms that thrive in these challenging environments are called extremophiles. Some of these draw directly upon the chemicals surrounding them for energy. Since these are very different forms of life than what we're used to, we may not think of them as alive, but they are.

HOW IT ALL WORKS

To try and understand how a living organism works, it helps to look at one example of its simplest form—the single-celled bacterium called *Streptococcus*. There are many kinds of these tiny organisms, and some are responsible for human illnesses. What makes us sick or uncomfortable are the toxins the bacteria give off in our bodies.

A single *Streptococcus* bacterium is so small that at least 500 of them could fit on the dot above this letter *i*. These bacteria are some of the simplest forms of life we know. They have no moving parts, no lungs, no brain, no heart, no liver, and no leaves or fruit. Yet this life-form reproduces. It grows in size by producing long chain structures, takes in nutrients, and gives off waste products. This tiny life-form is alive, just as you are alive.

What makes something alive is a question scientists grapple with when they study viruses, such as the ones that cause the common cold and smallpox. They can grow and reproduce within host cells, such as those that make up your body. Because viruses lack cells and cannot metabolize nutrients for energy or reproduce without a host, scientists ask if they are indeed alive. And don't go looking for them without a strong microscope—viruses are a hundred times smaller than bacteria.

Scientists think life began on Earth some 4.1 to 3.9 billion years ago, but no fossils exist from that time. The earliest fossils ever found are from the primitive life that existed 3.6 billion years ago. Other life-forms, some of which are shown below, soon followed. Scientists continue to study how life evolved on Earth and whether it is possible that life exists on other planets.

MICROSCOPIC ORGANISMS

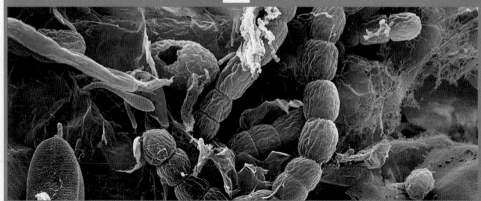

The Three Domains of Life

Biologists divide all living organisms into three domains: Bacteria, Archaea, and Eukarya. Archaean and Bacterial cells do not have nuclei, but they are so different from each other that they belong to different domains. Since human cells have a nucleus, humans belong to the Eukarya domain.

1

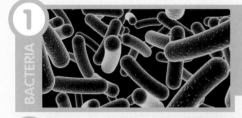

BACTERIA

DOMAIN BACTERIA: These single-celled microorganisms are found almost everywhere in the world. Bacteria are small and do not have nuclei. They can be shaped like rods, spirals, or spheres. Some of them are helpful to humans, and some are harmful.

2

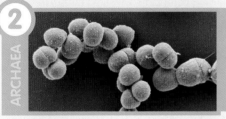

ARCHAEA

DOMAIN ARCHAEA: These single-celled micro-organisms are often found in extremely hostile environments. Like Bacteria, Archaea do not have nuclei, but they have some genes in common with Eukarya. For this reason, scientists think the Archaea living today most closely resemble the earliest forms of life on Earth.

3

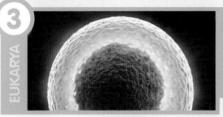

EUKARYA

DOMAIN EUKARYA: This diverse group of life-forms is more complicated than Bacteria and Archaea, as Eukarya have one or more cells with nuclei. These are the tiny cells that make up your whole body. Eukarya are divided into four groups: fungi, protists, plants, and animals.

WHAT IS A DOMAIN? Scientifically speaking, a domain is a major taxonomic division into which natural objects are classified (see p. 26 for "What Is Taxonomy?").

FYI

FUNGI

KINGDOM FUNGI (about 100,000 species): Mainly multicellular organisms, fungi cannot make their own food. Mushrooms and yeast are fungi.

PROTISTS

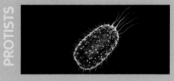

PROTISTS (about 250,000 species): Once considered a kingdom, this group is a "grab bag" that includes unicellular and multicellular organisms of great variety.

PLANTS

KINGDOM PLANTAE (about 400,000 species): Plants are multicellular, and many can make their own food using photosynthesis (see p. 86 for "Photosynthesis").

ANIMALS

KINGDOM ANIMALIA (about 1,000,000 species): Most animals, which are multi-cellular, have their own organ systems. Animals do not make their own food.

HOW DOES YOUR GARDEN GR🌻W?

The plant kingdom is about 400,000 species strong, growing all over the world: on top of mountains, in the sea, in frigid temperatures—everywhere. Without plants, life on Earth would not be able to survive. Plants provide food and oxygen for animals and humans.

Three characteristics make plants distinct:

1. Most have chlorophyll (a green pigment that makes photosynthesis work and turns sunlight into energy), while some are parasitic. These plants don't make their own food—they take it from other plants.

2. They cannot change their location on their own.

3. Their cell walls are made from a stiff material called cellulose.

Photosynthesis

Plants are lucky—most don't have to hunt or shop for food. Most use the sun to produce their own food. In a process called photosynthesis, a plant's chloroplast (the part of the plant where the chemical chlorophyll is located) captures the sun's energy and combines it with carbon dioxide from the air and nutrient-rich water from the ground to produce a sugar called glucose. Plants burn the glucose for energy to help them grow. As a waste product, plants emit oxygen, which humans and other animals need to breathe. When we breathe, we exhale carbon dioxide, which the plants then use for more photosynthesis—it's all a big, finely tuned system. So the next time you pass a lonely houseplant, give it thanks for helping you live.

Make a TERRARIUM

COLLECT MATERIALS FROM THE GREAT OUTDOORS

so you can enjoy nature when you're back inside. A terrarium is a great way to experiment with plants on a miniature level.

SUPPLY LIST

- Fishbowl or jar
- Activated charcoal
- Potting soil
- A variety of plants (miniature ferns or spider moss) or seeds (such as sweet alyssum or wheatgrass)
- Bits of nature from the outdoors, such as leaves, twigs, and mosses

STEPS

1. Wash and dry a large glass bowl or jar. (An old fishbowl works well.)
2. Fill the bottom—about 1 inch (2.5 cm) high—with stones you have collected from your nature hikes.
3. Using a shovel or spoon, add several inches of potting soil mixed with activated charcoal bits.
4. If you are using potted plants, dig a little hole in the soil for the roots and place the plants in. Pack extra soil around the plants. Add water until the soil is moist. (If you're using seeds, press them into the soil and moisten.)
5. Add sheet moss on top of the soil around the plants.
6. Now the fun part! Add a few decorative bits of nature—a small pinecone, a special rock, or a little figurine. Keep your terrarium in a well-lit place, and don't forget to add a little water when the soil looks dry.

Time: about 30 minutes

fun fact

Mosses grow in damp environments and are home to a little creature called a moss piglet! Moss piglets, also known as water bears, have eight legs and grow up to about .06 inch (1.5 mm) in length.

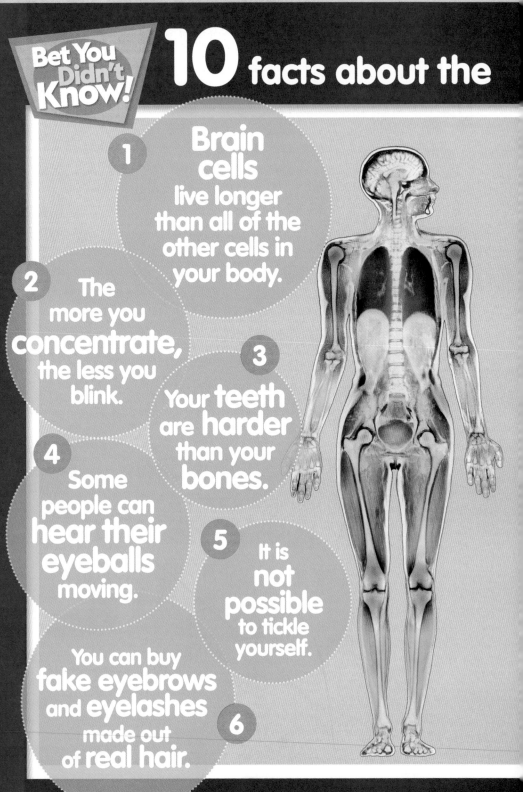

Bet You Didn't Know!

10 facts about the

1 **Brain cells** live longer than all of the other cells in your body.

2 **The more you concentrate,** the less you blink.

3 Your **teeth** are **harder** than your **bones.**

4 Some people can **hear their eyeballs** moving.

5 It is **not possible** to tickle yourself.

6 You can buy **fake eyebrows** and **eyelashes** made out of **real hair.**

human body

7 Fingernails grow **faster** than **toenails.**

8 Your heart beats about **100,000 times** each day.

9 **Your foot** is about the **same length** as the distance between your **elbow and wrist.**

10 The saliva you produce in your lifetime could fill nearly **30,000** water bottles.

MUSCLE POWER

With its strong bones and flexible joints, your skeleton is built to be on the go.

But without muscles, it won't go anywhere! You need muscle power to make your body walk, run, skip, rub your nose, or even just sit up without toppling over.

The muscles that do these jobs are called skeletal muscles. You have about 650 of them, and you can control what they do. Sometimes, it takes a lot of skeletal muscles to make even a simple move. Your tongue alone contains eight muscles!

You also have muscles that work without your having to do a thing. Most of these muscles are called smooth muscles. Sheets of smooth muscle line your blood vessels, throat, stomach, intestines, lungs, and other organs. They are hard at work keeping your blood circulating and your food digesting while you're busy doing other things. And there's also that mighty muscle, your heart. It pumps thanks to cardiac muscles, which are found only in the heart.

THE HIBERNATION MYSTERY

Very sick people often lie in bed for a long time as they recover. This lack of exercise weakens muscles—a process called "muscle atrophy." Preventing atrophy may be possible someday thanks to researchers who study hibernating animals.

Bears, for example, spend winter sleeping but do not suffer severe atrophy. When they wake up in spring, they're as strong as—well, bears! Scientists are studying the muscles and blood of bears, ground squirrels, and other hibernators to find out how they stay in shape while sleeping. The answers may one day help people suffering from muscle atrophy when they're sick or in the hospital for a long time.

Some of your body's strongest muscles aren't in your arms or legs. They're in your jaws! These strong muscles are called the masseters. They help you chew by closing your lower jaw. Clenching your teeth will make your masseters bulge so you can feel them.

BODY ELECTRIC

The nerve signal that tells your muscles to move is super fast! It zooms at 250 miles an hour (402 km/h), as fast as the fastest race car.

Your body is just humming with electricity.

Nerve cells from head to toe speak to each other through electrical signals. The electrical signals zap down each nerve cell and, when they get to the end, jump across a tiny gap called a synapse (see photo, right). How does the signal jump across the gap?

The nerve produces special chemicals that can flow across the gap to the next cell. There, a new electrical charge travels down the next nerve. Messages jump from neuron to neuron in a chain of electrical-chemical-electrical-chemical signals until they reach their destination.

Because nerves don't actually touch, they can change the path of their signals easily. They can make new connections and break old ones. This is how your brain learns and stores new information.

Bet You Didn't Know!

A reflex is a nerve message that doesn't go through your brain. When you touch a hot stove, for example, a sensory neuron picks up the message ("Hot!") and passes it to a motor neuron in your spinal cord. The motor neuron then sends a message to your hand, telling it to move ("Quick!").

BUNDLE OF NERVES

A 1.2-inch (3-cm) section of your brain stem (called the medulla oblongata) controls some of your body's most important functions, such as breathing and heart rate. Amazingly, it also contains your body's motor and sensory nerves and is where nerves from the left and right sides of your body cross each other on their journey toward your cerebrum.

SENSORY NERVES pull in information from nerve endings in your eyes, ears, skin, hands, and other parts of your body and then send this information to your brain.

MOTOR NERVES send messages from your brain to your muscles, telling them to contract, to run, or to walk.

LOOK OUT!

blood vessels

sclera

eyelash

retina

optic nerve

lens

pupil

conjunctiva

cornea

On a dark, clear night, it would be possible for you to see a car's headlights from about two miles (3.2 km) away.

Your eyes are two of the most amazing organs in your body.

These small, squishy, fluid-filled balls have almost three-quarters of your body's sensory receptors. They're like two supersmart cameras, but more complex.

So how do you see the world around you? It begins when you open the protective cover of your eyelid and let in the light. Light enters your eye through the window of your cornea and passes through the aqueous humor, a watery fluid that nourishes the eye tissue. It enters the black circle in the iris (the colored part of your eye), called the pupil. Because people need to be able to see in both bright and low light, muscles in the iris automatically make the pupil smaller when the light is strong and wider when the light is dim. Light then travels to the lens, whose muscles adjust it to be able to see objects both near and far. Then the light goes through the vitreous humor (a clear jellylike substance) to the retina. The retina, a layer of about 126 million light-sensitive cells, lines the back of your eyeball. When these cells absorb the light, they transform it into electrical signals that are sent along the optic nerve to the brain. The brain then makes sense of what you are seeing.

A TOPSY-TURVY WORLD

Turn this over in your mind: You're looking at the world topsy-turvy, and you don't even know it. Like a camera lens, your lens focuses light, creates an image, and turns it upside down.

Yep, when your lens focuses light inside your eye, it flips the image so it lands on your retina upside down. But, your brain knows to flip the image automatically to match your reality. But what if your reality suddenly changed? A well-known experiment in the mid-20th century in which a person wore special light-inverting goggles showed that his brain actually adjusted to the new, inverted world by eventually seeing the reversed view as normal! It is thought that newborns see the world upside down for a short while, until their brains learn how to turn things right-side up.

CAMERA LENS

AWESOME OPTICAL ILLUSIONS

Ready to work your brain and show your visual alertness?
Ponder these puzzling pictures to see what you see!

WHICH CIRCLE IS BIGGER?

Both of these circle clusters have an orange circle surrounded by purple ones. But which orange circle is bigger? The answer may surprise you: neither! The two orange circles are the same size. The one on the right may appear bigger because it's surrounded by purple circles that are smaller than it is. The one on the left seems smaller because it's surrounded by purple circles that are larger than it is.

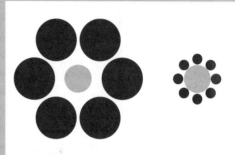

RABBIT OR DUCK?

It's a duck! Or is it a rabbit? Can you see it both ways? A recent study using this illusion suggests that the more easily people can switch back and forth between the two images, the more creative they are.

SPINNING CIRCLES

Do you see all the spinning circles? Don't look too long, or you might get dizzy! This illusion plays with your peripheral vision (vision from the sides of your eyes, not the middle). Sometimes when you look out the sides of your eyes, you see movement where really there are only patterns.

THE INVADERS ARE COMING!

BACTERIA

FUNGUS

VIRUS

PROTOZOA (CAN BE TRANSMITTED BY MOSQUITOES)

Every square inch (6.5 sq cm) of your skin hosts about **six million bacteria.**

Some microorganisms (tiny living things) can make your body sick. They are too small to see with the naked eye. These creatures—bacteria, viruses, fungi, and protozoa—are what you may know as germs.

Bacteria are microscopic organisms that live nearly everywhere on Earth, including on and in the human body. "Good" bacteria help sour digestive systems work properly. Harmful bacteria can cause ailments, including ear infections and strep throat.

A virus, like a cold or the flu, needs to live inside another living thing (a host) to survive; then it can grow and multiply throughout the host's body.

Fungi get their food from the plants, animals, or people they live on. Some fungi can get on your body and cause skin diseases such as ringworm.

Protozoa are single-celled organisms that can spread disease to humans through contaminated water and dirty living conditions. Protozoa can cause infections such as malaria, which occurs when a person is bitten by an infected mosquito.

ADD IT UP

So you know that you have bacteria on your skin and in your body. But do you know how many? One hundred trillion— that's 100,000,000,000,000! Most are harmless and some are pretty friendly, keeping more dangerous bacteria at bay, protecting you from some skin infections, and helping your cuts heal.

94

GERM **SHOWDOWN**

Scientists in Wales studied three greeting styles to determine which was the cleanest. Find out which one has the upper hand.

HANDSHAKE

AN AVERAGE HANDSHAKE TRANSFERRED **MORE THAN 5 TIMES AS MUCH BACTERIA** AS A FIST BUMP. (A STRONG HANDSHAKE TRANSFERRED **10 TIMES** AS MUCH.)

HIGH FIVE

A HIGH FIVE PASSED **TWICE AS MANY** GERMS AS A FIST BUMP.

FIST BUMP

WINNER:

FIST BUMPS HAVE THE **LEAST SKIN-TO-SKIN CONTACT** OF THE GREETINGS, WHICH MAKES IT LESS LIKELY FOR MICROBES TO JUMP **FROM ONE HAND TO ANOTHER.**

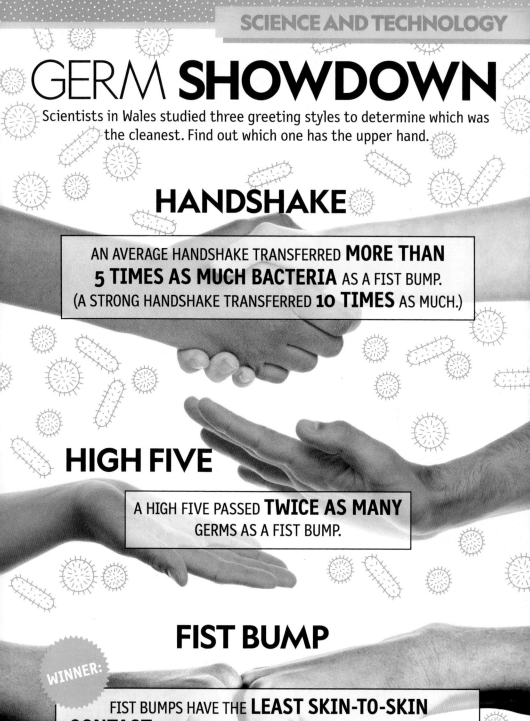

WHAT DIED?

CONCEPTS
decomposition,
microbiology, decay,
organic materials,
bacteria, insects,
corpse fauna

HOW LONG IT TAKES
two to four days, possibly
longer in cold weather

WHAT YOU NEED
food samples
containers
outdoor thermometer
magnifying lens
dissecting microscope
bug identification guides
optional: camera, smartphone,
or video camera

f you leave food out, SOMETHING
will come to live on it or lay eggs
on it. In this observation, discover
what arrives to make the most of
your leftovers.

What
comes to get
food that's
left out?

WHAT TO DO

DAY ONE:

1 WORK IN AN OPEN-AIR area, compost heap, or compost bin—a place that is open to bugs but not birds or other animals. Ask an adult to help you choose a location.

2 SET UP FOUR containers with a small sample of food inside each. If you want, these samples can represent the four food groups: vegetable/fruit, meat/fish, bread/grains, and milk/dairy.

DAYS TWO TO FOUR:

3 KEEP A CAREFUL record of what you observe through your senses. Each day, record the temperature in the area where your samples are. Note whether you can see signs that bugs or other creatures have been attracted to your samples, including any film or mold that forms. You may want to photograph the samples every day to compare them.

4 EVERY ONE OR TWO days (decide which interval you want to study), remove the samples from the containers to examine them with a magnifying lens and microscope. Count, try to identify, and sketch the bugs and other life-forms that colonize each sample. Add descriptions to your notes, including sensory observations: texture, color, and smell—but not taste!

WHAT TO EXPECT?
You may see mold, biofilm or scum, bugs, worms, flies, and so on.

WHAT'S GOING ON?
Nature abhors a vacuum. If there is food, something will come to eat it.

OUR TRY

We put out duplicate food—chicken broth, blackberry jam, and cat food—every other day for six days. We set out the food in the yard, in a cat carrier with a brick on top, but that didn't stop coyotes from pulling it apart and getting the food on the second night. After that we replaced the food and kept the cat carrier in the garage, where flies could still get to it. After we opened it to see what we had and examine it with the microscope, we dumped the cat carrier near the compost heap—and later, we had a glorious infestation of beetles.

QUESTION THIS!

- What would happen to this food if nothing were able to reach it?

- What would happen to this food if you let more time pass?

QUIZ WHIZ

Discover your tech-savvy smarts by taking this quiz!

Write your answers on a piece of paper. Then check them below.

1 How many plant species are there on Earth?

a. 400,000
b. 40,000
c. 4,000
d. 400

2 **True or false?** Some of your body's strongest muscles are in your jaw.

3 Microscopic organisms that live in moss are also known as _____.

a. moss monsters
b. moss piglets
c. moss monkeys
d. moss cows

4 **True or false?** Scientists think life began on Earth about 1 million years ago.

5 An architect has designed a conceptual floating island shaped like which object?

a. a lotus flower
b. a UFO
c. a lily pad
d. a roller coaster

Not **STUMPED** yet? Check out the *NATIONAL GEOGRAPHIC KIDS QUIZ WHIZ* collection for more crazy **TECHNOLOGY** questions!

ANSWERS:
1. a; 2. True (3. b.; 4. False. Experts think life began about four billion years ago; 5. c.

HOMEWORK HELP

This Is How It's Done!

Sometimes, the most complicated problems are solved with step-by-step directions. These "how-to" instructions are also known as a process analysis essay. While scientists and engineers use this tool to program robots and write computer code, you also use process analysis every day, from following a recipe to putting together a new toy or gadget. Here's how to write a basic process analysis essay.

Step 1: Choose Your Topic Sentence

Pick a clear and concise topic sentence that describes what you're writing about. Be sure to explain to the reader why the task is important—and how many steps there are to complete it.

Step 2: List Materials

Do you need specific ingredients or equipment to complete your process? Mention these right away so the readers will have all they need to do this activity.

Step 3: Write Your Directions

Your directions should be clear and easy to follow. Assume that you are explaining the process for the first time, and define any unfamiliar terms. List your steps in the exact order the reader will need to follow to complete the activity. Try to keep your essay limited to no more than six steps.

Step 4: Restate Your Main Idea

Your closing idea should revisit your topic sentence, drawing a conclusion relating to the importance of the subject.

EXAMPLE OF A PROCESS ANALYSIS ESSAY

Downloading an app is a simple way to enhance your tablet. Today, I'd like to show you how to search for and add an app to your tablet. First, you will need a tablet with the ability to access the internet. You'll also want to ask a parent for permission before you download anything onto your tablet. Next, select the specific app you're seeking by going to the app store on your tablet and entering the app's name into the search bar. Once you find the app you're seeking, select "download" and wait for the app to load. When you see that the app has fully loaded, tap on the icon and you will be able to access it. Now you can enjoy your app and have more fun with your tablet.

GOING GREEN

An artist's rendering offers a glimpse of the world's first forest city—scheduled for completion in 2020—along the Liujiang River in southern China. Buildings will be covered in thousands of trees and plants.

EARTH EXPLORER

Meet **Katey Walter Anthony!**

This aquatic ecologist and National Geographic explorer is tapping into new research on global warming.

Katey Walter Anthony remembers the first time she saw the bubbles. One day, while walking across a frozen lake in Siberia, she looked down and saw clusters of gas trapped beneath the thick, dark ice. "It looked like the starry night sky," Katey recalls.

But these weren't your average air bubbles. As Katey soon discovered, the bubbles were actually methane, a potent greenhouse gas that contributes to global warming. So how does the methane get under the ice? It comes from permafrost, the frozen ground that once covered the entire Arctic, including the bottom of ancient lakes that Katey studies. As the permafrost thaws from solid, frozen ground to looser soil and mud with Earth's rising temperatures, it can release carbon. Microbes in the soil turn the carbon into methane. In the summer, the gas rises up from the bottom of the lake, through the lake's surface, and enters the atmosphere. In the winter, it gets stuck under the frozen surface, creating those beautiful bubbles.

The way Katey determines whether the bubbles are methane is, well, pretty lit. "We tap holes into the ice and light a match," she says. "If there's methane and it mixes with oxygen, you'll get fireballs up to the trees."

As she's looked for methane in some 250 ancient lakes throughout Alaska and Russia, Katey has uncovered preserved woolly mammoth tusks and rhino bones. And she's also dug up proof that the methane being released from the melting permafrost is a source of climate change that many experts haven't recognized.

"Right now, if you look at the models of climate change, none of them include methane from thawing permafrost at the bottom of lakes as a source," says Katey. "We believe that the release of these gases intensifies global warming. It's a big part of the climate change story."

Siberian lakes have the potential to release an estimated 50 billion tons (45.4 billion t) of methane—10 times more methane than the atmosphere holds right now.

FROZEN METHANE BUBBLES

"All that carbon was locked up safely in the permafrost freezer for tens of thousands of years. Now the freezer door is opening, releasing the carbon into Arctic lake bottoms, where microbes convert it to methane."

Katey's team has studied 42,000-year-old methane gas.

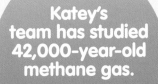

CALL TO ACTION!

"My wish for all kids is that you go out and explore nature," says Katey. "Be curious, study the world around you. And maybe that will help you one day make decisions that will help save the planet." You can also do your part to fight climate change through simple steps at home like recycling, powering down your electronics when you're not using them, and trying not to waste food.

KATEY CHECKING
BUBBLES FOR METHANE

Trapped by
TRASH!

VICTIM: SKUNK
TRASH: YOGURT CONTAINER
PROBLEM: HEAD STUCK

A HOMEOWNER finds a writhing baby skunk in her recycling bin. The skunk has a plastic yogurt container over his head. When the animal tries to push the container off, it won't budge. He claws at his head, struggling to free himself, then tumbles out of the uncovered bin. The panicked little skunk can't see a thing and begins to suffocate.

A PHONE CALL to Wildlife in Crisis, an animal rescue organization in nearby Weston, Connecticut, brings help. Director Dara Reid dispatches caretaker Anna Clark to the woman's home. She wraps the skunk in a towel and then gently tugs the container until the exhausted creature is finally free.

BUT HE'S NOT SAFE. There is no sign of the animal's mother, and this baby skunk is far too young to survive on his own. Wildlife in Crisis feeds him milk and wet cat food until his teeth grow in, and then adds natural foods like berries and worms to his diet. About four months later he's released into the wild.

Animals get trapped every day by the things people carelessly discard. Here are stories of lucky animals that have tangled with trash—and escaped.

VICTIM: SEA LION
TRASH: FISHING LINE
PROBLEM: MOUTH TRAPPED

The sea lion prowls for food off the California shore, sticking his nose in places where fish might hide. When his whiskers snag on some fishing line, he tries to shake it off. But the strong material tangles, wraps around his snout and neck, and eventually traps his mouth shut.

Someone notices the distressed animal and informs the Marine Mammal Center in nearby Sausalito. When the sea lion reappears in a bay, the center's rescue team speeds to the scene. The feisty sea lion eludes them for nearly three weeks.

The worried rescue team sedates him with darts while he rests on a dock. After he becomes sleepy, the team rushes the 260-pound (118-kg) mammal to the center to cut the fishing line, treat his wounds, and feed him. The sea lion eats 100 pounds (45 kg) of herring and is then set free. Hopefully now he steers clear of trash.

FISHING LINE

VICTIM: BALD EAGLE
TRASH: STRING
PROBLEM: WING TANGLED

A young bald eagle is in trouble. When her parents searched for sticks to build the nest, they also found balloon string, fishing line, and other trash. Now the young eagle is tangled in the debris and falls from the nest. The bird hangs four feet (1.2 m) above the ground, breaking her wing in the process.

Dara Reid of Wildlife in Crisis comes to the rescue. She cuts down the suspended eagle and rushes her to the rescue facility. After removing the trash, Reid aligns the bird's broken wing and immobilizes it by bandaging the wing against the eagle's body.

Following 14 months of TLC, the bald eagle is taken to a field. With a helpful heave from Reid, the eagle flaps hard, circles above, and then re-enters the wild—with a perfectly healed wing.

GETTING BETTER

FLYING AGAIN

A GLOBAL RACE TO ZERO WASTE

BOTH SWEDEN (MAIN PHOTO) AND SINGAPORE (INSET) ARE WORLDWIDE LEADERS IN RECYCLING AND WASTE REDUCTION.

It's an ambitious goal, but one that some countries hope to achieve in less than 10 years. The aim? Zero waste, meaning every single piece of trash will be reused or composted. The idea may seem impossible, but several spots are coming close.

Take Sweden, for example. Less than one percent of the country's household garbage ends up in landfills. Rather, the Swedes recycle nearly everything—some 1.5 billion bottles and cans annually—and the rest winds up at waste-to-energy plants to produce electricity. The program is so successful that Sweden actually imports trash from other places, such as the United Kingdom, Norway, and Ireland, to keep up the rapid pace of its incinerators.

Other places narrowing in on zero waste? The Himalayan country of Bhutan is shooting for that status by 2030, while Singapore and Dubai have announced similar timelines. In the United States, individual cities like San Francisco and New York have also declared their dedication to going zero waste. The U.S. National Park Service, as well as major corporations like Lego and Nike, are also making big moves toward creating zero waste—all in an effort to make this world a cleaner place.

So what's the secret to zero waste? It's all about enforcing the rules of reducing, reusing, and recycling. In Sweden, for example, recycling stations must be no more than 984 feet (300 m) from any residential area. And in Bhutan—which is aspiring to become the world's first nation to have an all-organic farming system—composting from food scraps is the norm. Simple practices like these, as well as educating the public on the problems stemming from too much trash, can lead to major changes. And, perhaps, zero waste around the world one day.

DUBAI—HOME TO THE FAMOUS PALM JUMEIRAH ISLAND—IS AIMING TO GO WASTE-FREE BY 2030.

FROM FILTH TO FASHION

Order up! One creative company called Garbage Gone Glam made this dress out of diner menus. Other things they've made? A cocktail dress out of playing cards and a ball gown out of old magazines!

HOW SOME TRASH TRAVELS FROM THE RECYCLING CENTER TO THE RUNWAYS—AND EVEN TO YOUR CLOSET.

A hat made out of an old soccer ball brings new meaning to the term "header."

This eco-friendly bag is made from 365 recycled computer keyboard keys.

This headpiece, made from recycled corrugated cardboard, is hard to top!

LEVI STRAUSS & CO. MAKES JEANS OUT OF OLD COTTON T-SHIRTS.

This bow tie made out of an old aluminum can is both fashion-forward and eco-friendly.

Pollution

Cleaning Up Our Act

So what's the big deal about a little dirt on the planet? Pollution can affect animals, plants, and people. In fact, some studies show that more people die every year from diseases linked to air pollution than from car accidents. And right now nearly one billion of the world's people don't have access to clean drinking water.

A LITTLE POLLUTION = BIG PROBLEMS
You can probably clean your room in a couple of hours. (At least we hope you can!) But you can't shove air and water pollution under your bed or cram them into the closet. Once released into the environment, pollution—whether it's oil leaking from a boat or chemicals spewing from a factory's smokestack—can have a lasting environmental impact.

KEEP IT CLEAN
It's easy to blame things like big factories for pollution problems. But some of the mess comes from everyday activities. Exhaust fumes from cars and garbage in landfills can seriously trash Earth's health. We all need to pitch in and do some housecleaning. It may mean bicycling more and riding in cars less. Or not dumping water-polluting oil or household cleaners down the drain. Look at it this way: Just as with your room, it's always better not to let Earth get messed up in the first place.

kids vs. PLASTIC

Part of the PLANET OR PLASTIC? initiative

A straw stuck in a sea turtle's nostril. A seahorse swimming along with its tail curled around a cotton swab. Sea birds washing up on sandy shores, entangled in plastic bags. Sadly, we do not have to look too far to see how animals are directly impacted by the staggering amount of plastic piling up on our planet. We've created more than 6.9 billion tons (6.3 billion t) of plastic waste, with only a small percentage landing in recycling bins. The rest of it lingers in landfills and winds up in our oceans. In fact, 700 species of animals are threatened because of ocean waste—and among seabirds, a whopping 90 percent eat plastic trash, according to a study. But as scary as these stats are, we can do something about them. Experts say it all starts with reducing the amount of plastic we use, including options for reusable containers or those made with marine biodegradable components. You can also pledge to do your part to reduce the plastic problem by visiting kids.nationalgeographic.com/explore/nature/kids-vs-plastic. Together, we can work to cut back on plastic and protect our planet—and everything on it.

Declining Biodiversity

Saving All Creatures, Great and Small

Earth is home to a huge mix of plants and animals—millions and possibly billions of species—and scientists have officially identified and named only about 1.9 million so far! Scientists call this healthy mix biodiversity.

THE BALANCING ACT

The bad news is that half of the planet's plant and animal species may be on the path to extinction, mainly because of human activity. People cut down trees, build roads and houses, pollute rivers, overfish, and overhunt. The good news is that many people care. Scientists and volunteers race against the clock every day, working to save wildlife before time runs out. By building birdhouses, planting trees, and following the rules for hunting and fishing, you can be a positive force for preserving biodiversity, too. Every time you do something to help a species survive, you help our planet to thrive.

Green sea turtle

Habitats Threatened

Living on the Edge

Even though tropical rain forests cover only about 7 percent of the planet's total land surface, they are home to half of all known species of plants and animals. Because people cut down so many trees for lumber and firewood and clear so much land for farms, hundreds of thousands of acres of rain forest disappear every year.

SHARING THE LAND

Wetlands are also important feeding and breeding grounds. People have drained many wetlands, turning them into farm fields or sites for industries. More than half the world's wetlands have disappeared within the past century, squeezing wildlife out. Balancing the needs of humans and animals is the key to lessening habitat destruction.

Jaguar

WORLD ENERGY & MINERALS

Almost everything people do—from cooking to powering the International Space Station—requires energy. But energy comes in different forms. Traditional energy sources, still used by many people in the developing world, include burning dried animal dung and wood. Industrialized countries and urban centers around the world rely on coal, oil, and natural gas—called fossil fuels because they formed from decayed plant and animal material accumulated from long ago. Fossil fuel deposits, either in the ground or under the ocean floor, are unevenly distributed on Earth, and only some countries can afford to buy them. Fossil fuels are also not renewable, meaning they will run out one day. And unless we find other ways to create energy, we'll be stuck. Without energy we won't be able to drive cars, use lights, or send emails to friends.

TAKING A TOLL

Environmentally speaking, burning fossil fuels isn't necessarily the best choice, either: Carbon dioxide from the burning of fossil fuels, as well as other emissions, are contributing to global warming. Concerned scientists are looking at new ways to harness renewable, alternative sources of energy, such as water, wind, and sun.

HIGH VOLTAGE

5% OTHER, SUCH AS GEOTHERMAL, SOLAR, WIND, HEAT, ETC.

5% OIL

10.9% NUCLEAR

16.2% HYDRO POWER

It seems like we use electricity for everything——from TVs and cell phones to air conditioners and computers. In fact, power plants generate 3.7 times more electrical power than they did just 40 years ago. How they do this can differ around the world. Is it from burning coal or taming the energy in moving water? Here's the global breakdown.

40.4% COAL

22.5% NATURAL GAS

Electricity travels at the speed of light—about 186,000 miles a second (299,340 km/s).

Climate CHANGE

POLAR BEAR ON A PIECE OF MELTING ICEBERG

Rising Temperatures, Explained

Fact: The world is getting warmer.
Earth's surface temperature has been increasing. In the past 50 years, our planet has warmed twice as fast as in the 50 years before that. This is the direct effect of climate change, which refers not only to the increase in Earth's average temperature (known as global warming), but also to the long-term effects on winds, rain, and ocean currents. Global warming is the reason glaciers and polar ice sheets are melting—resulting in rising sea levels and shrinking habitats. This makes survival for some animals a big challenge. Warming also means more flooding along the coasts and drought for inland areas.

Why are temperatures climbing?
Some of the recent climate changes can be tied to natural causes—such as changes in the sun's intensity, the unusually warm ocean currents

SCIENTISTS ARE CONCERNED THAT GREENLAND'S ICE SHEET HAS BEGUN TO MELT IN SUMMER. BIRTHDAY CANYON, SHOWN HERE, WAS CARVED BY MELTWATER.

of El Niño, and volcanic activity—but human activities are a major factor as well.

Everyday activities that require burning fossil fuels, such as driving gasoline-powered cars, contribute to global warming. These activities produce greenhouse gases, which enter the atmosphere and trap heat. At the current rate, Earth's global average temperature is projected to rise between 1.8 and 11.5°F (1 and 6.4°C) by the year 2100, and it will get even warmer after that. And as the climate continues to warm, it will unfortunately continue to affect the environment and our society in many ways.

FUNKY JUNK ART

Try This!

Who knew recycling could be so much fun? Check out these ideas for turning junk into awesome art.

Bottle Cap Snake

> ASK FOR A PARENT'S HELP AND PERMISSION BEFORE YOU START THESE PROJECTS.

YOU WILL NEED
- 30–50 BOTTLE CAPS
- HAMMER
- AWL
- BOARD (TO HAMMER ON)
- PLASTIC-COATED WIRE
- CRAFT GLUE
- SELF-HARDENING CLAY
- 1 CORK
- 2 PUSHPINS

WHAT TO DO

Work with a parent to punch a hole in the center of each bottle cap using a hammer and awl. Do this on a board that is resting on a sturdy surface. Cut a piece of wire that is slightly longer than you want your snake to be. Tie a knot at one end of the wire. String all the bottle caps on the wire with the tops facing the open end of the wire. Knot the other end of the wire and cut off the excess. Glue a piece of clay to the snake's tail end and twist it into a tail shape. Glue a piece of clay to the opposite end of the snake. Create an indentation with the cork. Let the clay dry. Glue the cork into the clay. Once dry, press pushpins into the cork for eyes and some wire into the end of the cork for the tongue. Glue a piece of clay to the cork tip.

Create a College

Cut up magazines or the Sunday comics and glue the pictures onto construction paper to make a funny collage.

Toy Mosaic

YOU WILL NEED
- OLD TOYS, COLORED GLASS, STONES, BUTTONS, SHELLS, OR OTHER SMALL ITEMS
- THICK WHITE POSTER BOARD
- CRAFT GLUE
- THICK BLACK POSTER BOARD

WHAT TO DO
Collect small decorative items (see suggestions above) from around your house. Sketch a pattern for your collage on a piece of white poster board. Glue all of the pieces on top of the pattern. Let the glue dry. Cut a piece of heavy black poster board that is two inches (5 cm) wider on all sides than the white poster board. Center the white piece on the black one and glue it in place. Let the glue dry, then put your masterpiece on display for everyone to see.

Hang Your Name

Find the letters of your name in old posters or catalogs and cut them out. Glue the letters to cardboard that's covered with paper. Tape your nameplate to your bedroom door.

10 WAYS YOU CAN GO GREEN!

WANT TO DO YOUR PART TO SAVE THE PLANET? HERE ARE 10 THINGS TO TRY TODAY!

1 **Use rechargeable batteries**, and recycle them when they die to keep harmful metals from entering the environment.

2 **Never litter.** Trash tossed carelessly outside often winds up in storm drains, which empty into rivers and streams that eventually flow to the oceans.

3 **Plant a deciduous (leafy) tree** that loses its leaves in the fall on the south side of your home. When it grows tall, its shade will cool your house in the summer. After its leaves fall, sunlight will help warm your house in winter.

4 **Reuse or recycle plastic bags.** When one ton (0.9 t) of plastic bags is reused or recycled, the energy equivalent of 11 barrels of oil is saved!

5 **Donate your old clothes** and toys to reduce waste.

6 **Take shorter showers** to save water.

7 **Switch off the light** every time you leave a room.

8 **Participate in cleanup days** at your school or at a park—or organize one on your own.

9 **Place your desk next to a window** and use natural light instead of a lamp.

10 **Have a drippy faucet at home?** Ask your parents to replace the washer inside it to save water.

QUIZ WHIZ

What's your eco-friendly IQ? Find out with this quiz!

Write your answers on a piece of paper. Then check them below.

1 **True or false?** The country of Sweden recycles some 1.5 billion bottles and cans annually.

2 **What does global warming cause?**
a. rising sea levels
b. shrinking animal habitats
c. melting glaciers
d. all of the above

3 **Electricity travels at about the same rate as what?**
a. sound
b. light
c. Wi-Fi
d. a sloth

4 **True or false?** Hundreds of thousands of acres of rain forest disappear every year.

5 **700 species of animals are severely threatened because of _____ waste.**
a. ocean
b. food
c. electronic
d. paper

Not **STUMPED** yet? Check out the *NATIONAL GEOGRAPHIC KIDS QUIZ WHIZ* collection for more crazy **ENVIRONMENT** questions

ANSWERS: 1. True ; 2. d ; 3. b ; 4. True; 5. a

Write a Letter That Gets Results

Knowing how to write a good letter is a useful skill. It will come in handy anytime you want to persuade someone to understand your point of view. Whether you're emailing your congressperson or writing a letter for a school project or to your grandma, a great letter will help you get your message across. Most important, a well-written letter leaves a good impression.

CHECK OUT THE EXAMPLE BELOW FOR THE ELEMENTS OF A GOOD LETTER.

Your address

Date

Salutation
Always use "Dear" followed by the person's name; use Mr., Mrs., Ms., or Dr. as appropriate.

Introductory paragraph
Give the reason you're writing the letter.

Body
The longest part of the letter, which provides evidence that supports your position. Be persuasive!

Closing paragraph
Sum up your argument.

Complimentary closing
Sign off with "Sincerely" or "Thank you."

Your signature

Abby Jones
1204 Green Street
Los Angeles, CA 90045

April 22, 2020

Dear Ms. School Superintendent,

I am writing to you about how much excess energy our school uses and to offer a solution.

Every day, we leave the computers on in the classroom. The TVs are plugged in all the time, and the lights are on all day. All of this adds up to a lot of wasted energy, which is not only harmful for the Earth, as it increases the amount of harmful greenhouse gas emissions into the environment, but is also costly to the school. In fact, I read that schools spend more on energy bills than on computers and textbooks combined!

I am suggesting that we start an Energy Patrol to monitor the use of lighting, air-conditioning, heating, and other energy systems within our school. My idea is to have a group of students dedicated to figuring out ways we can cut back on our energy use in the school. We can do room checks, provide reminders to students and teachers to turn off lights and computers, replace old lightbulbs with energy-efficient products, and even reward the classrooms that do the most to save energy.

Above all, I think our school could help the environment tremendously by cutting back on how much energy we use. Let's see an Energy Patrol at our school soon. Thank you.

Sincerely,

Abby Jones

Abby Jones

COMPLIMENTARY CLOSINGS

Sincerely, Sincerely yours, Thank you, Regards, Best wishes, Respectfully,

Inca dancers perform in traditional dress in the Cusco region of Peru.

CULTURE
CONNECTION

This National Geographic explorer-in-residence makes it her mission to tell the stories of different cultures around the world.

As a little girl growing up in Hawaii, Elizabeth Kapu'uwailani Lindsey watched her elders—the older women who looked after her—pay close attention to signs in nature to gain a better understanding of the world around them. "They didn't rely on their smartphones to tell them the weather forecast," she explains. "Instead, they watched the clouds, felt the winds, and looked at the color of the sky. The simple task of observing what's going on around you can teach you so much."

Today, Elizabeth is an anthropologist who travels the world to study indigenous—or native—people who still follow ancient traditions, like the adults she grew up with. Her purpose? To keep these cultures from vanishing.

"Their cultures are often misunderstood and forced to blend into mainstream society," she says. "Instead, why not learn more about them and understand that they are just a part of our planet?"

Elizabeth has spent time with Southeast Asian sea nomads and with native people of New Zealand, Peru, China, Micronesia, and India, among others. She has also studied wayfinding—or the native science of navigating without tools, most recently featured in the movie *Moana*.

"Wayfinders don't use maps," Elizabeth explains. "They look at everything from ocean waves to the flight patterns of birds to get to where they need to go. Their approach is that if you gather enough information from the world around you, you essentially find your way home."

Elizabeth is hoping to discover a complete story of the peoples of the world, with each culture representing a chapter.

"We are alive at an age when there are still elders whose wisdom is available," she says. "I look for the lessons we can learn from their ancient wisdom and knowledge. This way, we can be sure their voices are heard for many more years to come. If one voice is missing, the story is incomplete."

There are at least 8 different languages spoken in Micronesia, a country in the Pacific Ocean.

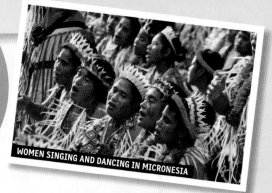

WOMEN SINGING AND DANCING IN MICRONESIA

" Wayfinders look at nature to know where they are. The underbellies of the clouds are like mirrors and reflect colors. When you're on the ocean and you can see the palest color of green in the clouds, you know you're getting close to land. Little clues help them find their way. "

BOATS OF THE MOKEN TRIBE IN SOUTHERN THAILAND

CALL TO ACTION!

Be curious! Seek out information about traditions in your own family and learn their importance. Talk to your parents, grandparents, aunts, and uncles about what makes your family's history unique. Gather as many details as you can and share them. That way you can carry on traditions from one generation to another.

Maui, the famous demigod from the movie *Moana,* is based on a legend from traditional Polynesian stories passed down from generation to generation.

CELEBRATIONS

1

CHINESE NEW YEAR
January 25
Also called Lunar New Year, this holiday marks the new year according to the lunar calendar. Families celebrate with parades, feasts, and fireworks. Young people may receive gifts of money in red envelopes.

2
HOLI
March 9
This festival in India celebrates spring and marks the triumph of good over evil. People cover one another with powdered paint, called *gulal*, and douse one another with buckets of colored water.

3
NYEPI
March 25
A national day of silence, this Hindu holiday marks Lunar New Year in Bali, Indonesia, and encourages meditation and reflection. Those who follow traditional customs do not talk, use electricity, travel, or eat for 24 hours.

4
QINGMING FESTIVAL
April 4
Also known as Grave Sweeping Day, this Chinese celebration calls on people to return to the graves of their deceased loved ones. There, they tidy up the graves, as well as light firecrackers, burn fake money, and leave food as an offering to the spirits.

5
EASTER
April 12
A Christian holiday that honors the resurrection of Jesus Christ, Easter is celebrated by giving baskets filled with gifts, decorated eggs, or candy to children.

6
VESAK DAY
April or May, date varies by country
Buddhists around the world observe Buddha's birthday with rituals including chanting and prayer, candlelight processions, and meditation.

7
RAMADAN AND EID AL-FITR
April 23*–May 24**
A Muslim holiday, Ramadan is a month long, ending in the Eid al-Fitr celebration. Observers fast during this month—eating only after sunset. People pray for forgiveness and hope to purify themselves through observance.

8
BERMUDA DAY
May 29
The first day of the year that Bermudians take a dip in the ocean. It is also traditionally the first day on which Bermuda shorts are worn as business attire. To celebrate the holiday, there is a parade in Hamilton, and a road race from the west end of the island into Hamilton.

9
ST. JOHN'S NIGHT
June 23
In Poland, people celebrate the longest day of the year—also known as the summer solstice—with rituals including bonfires, floating flower wreaths down a stream, and releasing thousands of paper lanterns into the night sky.

10
BORYEONG MUD FESTIVAL
July
During the Boryeong Mud Festival in South Korea, people swim, slide, and wrestle in the mud, then kick back and relax to music and fireworks.

*Begins at sundown.
**Dates may vary slightly by location.

Around the World

11 LA TOMATINA

August 26

Close to 250,000 pounds (113,000 kg) of tomatoes are hurled during this annual event in the Spanish town of Buñol. The festivities involve more than 20,000 people, making this one of the world's largest food fights.

12 MASSKARA FESTIVAL

October

Celebrated in Bacolod, Philippines, this relatively young holiday was established in 1980 to promote happiness. People dance in the streets wearing colorful costumes and smiley-face masks.

13 ROSH HASHANAH

September 18*–20

A Jewish holiday marking the beginning of a new year on the Hebrew calendar. Celebrations include prayer, ritual foods, and a day of rest.

14 HANUKKAH

December 10*–18

This Jewish holiday is eight days long. It commemorates the rededication of the Temple in Jerusalem. Hanukkah celebrations include the lighting of menorah candles for eight days and the exchange of gifts.

15 CHRISTMAS DAY

December 25

A Christian holiday marking the birth of Jesus Christ, Christmas is usually celebrated by decorating trees, exchanging presents, and having festive gatherings.

2020 CALENDAR

JANUARY

S	M	T	W	T	F	S
			1	2	3	4
5	6	7	8	9	10	11
12	13	14	15	16	17	18
19	20	21	22	23	24	25
26	27	28	29	30	31	

FEBRUARY

S	M	T	W	T	F	S
						1
2	3	4	5	6	7	8
9	10	11	12	13	14	15
16	17	18	19	20	21	22
23	24	25	26	27	28	29

MARCH

S	M	T	W	T	F	S
1	2	3	4	5	6	7
8	9	10	11	12	13	14
15	16	17	18	19	20	21
22	23	24	25	26	27	28
29	30	31				

APRIL

S	M	T	W	T	F	S
			1	2	3	4
5	6	7	8	9	10	11
12	13	14	15	16	17	18
19	20	21	22	23	24	25
26	27	28	29	30		

MAY

S	M	T	W	T	F	S
					1	2
3	4	5	6	7	8	9
10	11	12	13	14	15	16
17	18	19	20	21	22	23
24	25	26	27	28	29	30
31						

JUNE

S	M	T	W	T	F	S
	1	2	3	4	5	6
7	8	9	10	11	12	13
14	15	16	17	18	19	20
21	22	23	24	25	26	27
28	29	30				

JULY

S	M	T	W	T	F	S
			1	2	3	4
5	6	7	8	9	10	11
12	13	14	15	16	17	18
19	20	21	22	23	24	25
26	27	28	29	30	31	

AUGUST

S	M	T	W	T	F	S
						1
2	3	4	5	6	7	8
9	10	11	12	13	14	15
16	17	18	19	20	21	22
23	24	25	26	27	28	29
30	31					

SEPTEMBER

S	M	T	W	T	F	S
		1	2	3	4	5
6	7	8	9	10	11	12
13	14	15	16	17	18	19
20	21	22	23	24	25	26
27	28	29	30			

OCTOBER

S	M	T	W	T	F	S
				1	2	3
4	5	6	7	8	9	10
11	12	13	14	15	16	17
18	19	20	21	22	23	24
25	26	27	28	29	30	31

NOVEMBER

S	M	T	W	T	F	S
1	2	3	4	5	6	7
8	9	10	11	12	13	14
15	16	17	18	19	20	21
22	23	24	25	26	27	28
29	30					

DECEMBER

S	M	T	W	T	F	S
		1	2	3	4	5
6	7	8	9	10	11	12
13	14	15	16	17	18	19
20	21	22	23	24	25	26
27	28	29	30	31		

DIWALI

FLAMES FROM OIL LAMPS flicker as families gather together to share music, food, and gifts in the spirit of Diwali, often called the Festival of Lights. This Hindu holiday, celebrating the triumph of good over evil and the lifting of spiritual darkness, is actually a series of festivals: Each of the five days of Diwali honors a different tradition. Diwali customs include cleaning and decorating houses and wearing new clothes.

Women in Chandigarh, India, light lamps on the eve of Diwali.

Carnival celebration in Salvador, Brazil

CARNIVAL

COLORFUL COSTUMES, festive music, parades, and parties for days—sounds fun, huh? One of the biggest bashes around the world, Carnival originated as a way for Catholics to mark the last days before Lent, the period of fasting before Easter. Thousands of partyers also take to the streets each spring, especially in the Caribbean country of Trinidad and Tobago and throughout South America. The hottest place to celebrate at Carnival time? Salvador, Brazil, considered one of the biggest street parties on the planet!

What's Your Chinese Horoscope?
Locate your birth year to find out.

In Chinese astrology the zodiac runs on a 12-year cycle, based on the lunar calendar. Each year corresponds to one of 12 animals, each representing one of 12 personality types. Read on to find out which animal year you were born in and what that might say about you.

RAT
1972, '84, '96, 2008, '20
Say cheese! You're attractive, charming, and creative. When you get mad, you can have really sharp teeth!

HORSE
1966, '78, '90, 2002, '14
Being happy is your "mane" goal. And while you're smart and hardworking, your teacher may ride you for talking too much.

OX
1973, '85, '97, 2009, '21
You're smart, patient, and as strong as an ... well, you know what. Though you're a leader, you never brag.

SHEEP
1967, '79, '91, 2003, '15
Gentle as a lamb, you're also artistic, compassionate, and wise. You're often shy.

TIGER
1974, '86, '98, 2010
You may be a nice person, but no one should ever enter your room without asking—you might attack!

MONKEY
1968, '80, '92, 2004, '16
No "monkey see, monkey do" for you. You're a clever problem-solver with an excellent memory.

RABBIT
1975, '87, '99, 2011
Your ambition and talent make you jump at opportunity. You also keep your ears open for gossip.

ROOSTER
1969, '81, '93, 2005, '17
You crow about your adventures, but inside you're really shy. You're thoughtful, capable, brave, and talented.

DRAGON
1976, '88, 2000, '12
You're on fire! Health, energy, honesty, and bravery make you a living legend.

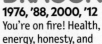

DOG
1970, '82, '94, 2006, '18
Often the leader of the pack, you're loyal and honest. You can also keep a secret.

SNAKE
1977, '89, 2001, '13
You may not speak often, but you're very smart. You always seem to have a stash of cash.

PIG
1971, '83, '95, 2007, '19
Even though you're courageous, honest, and kind, you never hog all the attention.

HALLOWEEN PET PARADE

What spell can I cast to get some oats and hay?

DISGUISED AS HARRY POTTER, RAMSEY THE HORSE MAKES MAGIC.

Stop in the name of the paw, er, law!

COREY THE DACHSHUND IS ARRESTING IN HIS WILD WEST SHERIFF GARB.

I'm ready to say "I do" to a chew toy and a belly rub.

TANK THE ENGLISH BULLDOG ROCKS A BRIDAL COSTUME.

I am one classy kitty.

ELROY THE CAT SHOWS SOME STYLE DRESSED AS THE MAD HATTER FROM *ALICE'S ADVENTURES IN WONDERLAND*.

Cool Carvings

Show your pumpkin's true personality with these wacky designs. Use a child-safe carving tool or ask an adult for help.

Express Yourself!

Let your jack-o'-lantern tell the world how it feels with emoticon smileys. It'll make your friends LOL!

Ahoy, Matey!

Pumpkins can wear costumes, too. Hats, inexpensive jewelry, and other accessories can create a pirate, cowboy, or even a baseball player.

Spell It Out

Who says a jack-o'-lantern needs a face? Carve spooky messages into your pumpkins instead.

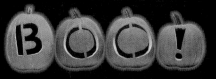

Stack 'Em Up

Build a snowman by placing the biggest pumpkin at the bottom and the smallest one on top. Slant the knife when you cut off the tops, creating a ledge to support another pumpkin.

CREATE THE **PERFECT** DESIGN

Before you start cutting, sketch your design on white paper. Tape the paper to your pumpkin where you want the design to be. Punch along the lines of the sketch with a pin, poking through the paper and into the pumpkin. Then carve along the dotted lines you've made on the pumpkin.

125

CHEW ON THIS

TACOS!
The word "taco" hasn't always been on restaurant menus. In the 18th century, "tacos" were charges of gunpowder wrapped in paper used by Mexican miners. The wrap concept stuck when cooks started calling tortillas stuffed with meat and beans "tacos." Chow down on more filling facts.

People in the United States spend more money on **SALSA** than on ketchup.

Made from avocado, **GUACAMOLE** comes from the Aztec word *ahuacamolli* (ah-wah-kah-MOH-lee), or avocado sauce.

Natural **CHEDDAR CHEESE** has an almost white color. The bright orange color you see in grocery store cheddar comes from food coloring.

Crunchy corn **TACO** shells have been in U.S. cookbooks only since 1939. But soft tortillas have been around since the 13th century.

One type of **BLACK BEAN** tastes like mushrooms.

MAKE YOUR OWN TACOS

Tacos are crunchy sandwiches—the tortilla is like the bread, which you can stuff with anything you want! Get a parent's help to create a yummy taco.

1 Warm a skillet over medium heat. Cook 1½ pounds (680 g) ground beef or turkey for 6 to 8 minutes.

2 Add 1 teaspoon (2 g) cumin and ¾ teaspoon (4 g) salt. Stir occasionally for 2 to 3 minutes.

3 Fill 8 taco shells with the meat and top with diced avocado, sour cream, black beans, and salsa.

4 Sprinkle with cheddar cheese.

PIZZA!

Pizza may have originated 2,000 years ago when the ancient Greeks prepared round, flat breads covered with oil, herbs, and spices. In 1830, chefs in Naples, Italy, cooked their crust in an oven lined with rocks from a nearby volcano. Some say that could have been the first pizzeria. The restaurant is still open today. Gobble up these other tasty tidbits.

MUSHROOMS are some seriously freaky fungi. They've been grown in caves and buried in, um, excrement, and some even glow in the dark.

People in the United States eat about 250 million pounds (113 million kg) of **PEPPERONI** a year, more than any other pizza topping.

BELL PEPPERS are fruits, not vegetables.

Most **CHEESE** is made from cow's, goat's, or sheep's milk. The traditional way to make mozzarella is from water buffalo's milk.

TOMATOES can be red, orange, yellow, green, purple, and even striped.

13 x .5 in

MAKE YOUR OWN PIZZA

Created in Naples, Italy, the Margherita pizza represents the colors in the Italian flag: red tomatoes, green basil, and white cheese. Get a parent's help to make your own Margherita pizza, or use toppings like mushrooms and bell peppers to make a new tasty creation!

1 Bake premade pizza dough at 450°F (232°C) for about 5 minutes. Brush the crust lightly with olive oil.

2 Top dough with 4 or 5 thin tomato slices, and a pinch each of dried oregano, salt, and pepper. Sprinkle 1 cup (125 g) shredded mozzarella on top.

3 Bake until golden for 10 to 12 minutes. Sprinkle ½ cup (20 g) chopped fresh basil over the top.

MONEY AROUND THE WORLD!

Jordan's HALF-DINAR COIN has seven sides.

ACCORDING to some **PEOPLE, CANADA'S $100 BANKNOTE** gives off the scent of **MAPLE SYRUP.**

A British businessman created his own currency —named the **PUFFIN—** for an island he owned off of England.

IN FEBRUARY 2015 SCUBA DIVERS **OFF ISRAEL FOUND OVER 2,600** GOLD **COINS DATING BACK AS FAR AS THE 9TH CENTURY.**

A **20,000**-PESO BANKNOTE FROM CHILE CONTAINS INK THAT CHANGES **COLOR WHEN TILTED.**

The **INCA** called gold "THE SWEAT OF THE SUN" and silver "THE TEARS OF THE MOON."

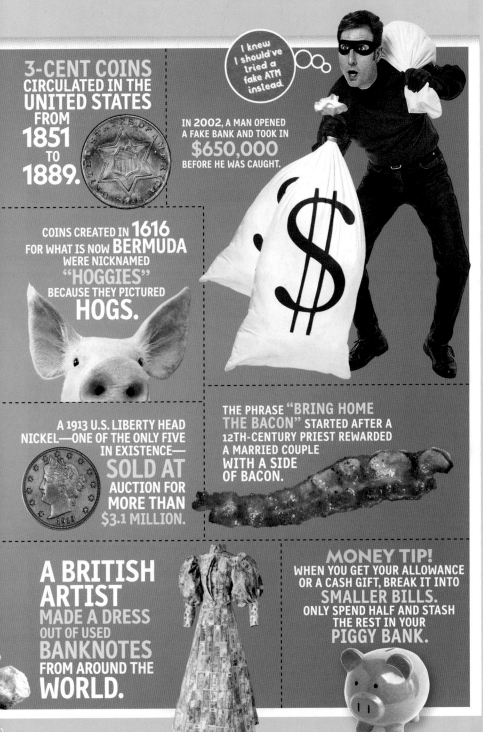

3-CENT COINS CIRCULATED IN THE **UNITED STATES** FROM **1851** TO **1889.**

I knew I should've tried a fake ATM instead.

IN 2002, A MAN OPENED A FAKE BANK AND TOOK IN **$650,000** BEFORE HE WAS CAUGHT.

COINS CREATED IN **1616** FOR WHAT IS NOW **BERMUDA** WERE NICKNAMED **"HOGGIES"** BECAUSE THEY PICTURED **HOGS.**

A 1913 U.S. LIBERTY HEAD NICKEL—ONE OF THE ONLY FIVE IN EXISTENCE— **SOLD AT** AUCTION FOR MORE THAN $3.1 MILLION.

THE PHRASE "BRING HOME THE BACON" STARTED AFTER A 12TH-CENTURY PRIEST REWARDED A MARRIED COUPLE WITH A SIDE OF BACON.

A BRITISH ARTIST MADE A DRESS OUT OF USED **BANKNOTES** FROM AROUND THE **WORLD.**

MONEY TIP! WHEN YOU GET YOUR ALLOWANCE OR A CASH GIFT, BREAK IT INTO **SMALLER BILLS.** ONLY SPEND HALF AND STASH THE REST IN YOUR **PIGGY BANK.**

CRAFTS AROUND THE GLOBE

Try This!

Try these fun activities inspired by different cultures

Ask for a parent's help and permission before you start these projects.

FUN FACT
Trolls are part of Norway's folklore. Legend has it that these creatures of the dark turn to stone if they're caught in the sun.

TROLL DOLLS

YOU WILL NEED
- GLUE
- FELT AND/OR FABRIC
- SMALL PLASTIC BOTTLE SUCH AS A SPICE JAR
- FAKE FUR
- GOOGLY EYES
- DECORATIONS SUCH AS YARN, STICKERS, AND PAPER CUTOUTS

WHAT TO DO
Decide what characters you want to make and pick out the materials you need at a craft store. Glue felt around the bottle where the face will go. Glue the fake fur along the top edge of the felt so it stands up straight. Then glue on the fabric "clothing," googly eyes, and your choice of decorations and accessories. Be sure to let each layer dry before adding the next layer of material.

FUN FACT
Navajo Indians create sandpaintings as part of healing ceremonies and other rituals.

SANDPAINTING

YOU WILL NEED
- CANVAS BOARD OR FOAM BOARD
- GLUE
- COLORED SAND (AVAILABLE IN CRAFT STORES)
- PENCIL AND BLACK MARKER

WHAT TO DO
Sketch your design on the board in pencil. When you are happy with the sketch, outline it with the marker. Starting at the top, cover a small area with glue and then one color of sand. Make sure you don't get glue and sand on the marker lines. Shake excess sand back into the container and let the glue dry. Repeat using different colors for different areas. Dry overnight.

TIE-DYED T-SHIRT

YOU WILL NEED
- WHITE, 100% COTTON T-SHIRT (PREWASHED)
- RUBBER BANDS
- LARGE POT
- HOT WATER
- FABRIC DYE (ANY COLOR)
- LARGE BUCKET
- TONGS
- WATER- AND HEAT-SAFE RUBBER GLOVES

CAUTION! Dye can stain anything, even the sink. Cover your work area with plastic and read the cleaning instructions on the dye package. Always wear rubber gloves.

FUN FACT
Japanese tie-dye, or *shibori*, is more than 1,000 years old. Peasants used the technique to brighten up old clothes. Tie-dye was also fashionable among royalty.

WHAT TO DO
1. Dampen the T-shirt. For a random pattern, twist and scrunch the fabric, using rubber bands to hold the T-shirt in that position. For a circular pattern like the one at right, grab part of the T-shirt and squeeze it into a long, skinny shape. Tie several equally spaced rubber bands around the fabric. Each rubber band will form a circle.

2. Ask a parent to boil water in the large pot. Using the measurements on the dye package, ask your parent to pour the hot water into a bucket and stir in the dye.

3. Dunk the shirt into the water with the tongs and stir constantly for about 10 to 15 minutes. (The T-shirt appears slightly darker when it's wet.)

4. Rinse the shirt under cold water. Then remove the rubber bands and rinse until the water runs clear. Dry in a clothes dryer to help set the color.

15 Ways to Say Hello

1. ARMENIAN: Barev
2. DUTCH: Goedendag
3. FINNISH: Hei
4. FRENCH: Bonjour
5. GREEK: Yia sou
6. HEBREW: Shalom
7. HINDI: Namaste
8. ICELANDIC: Halló
9. ITALIAN: Ciao
10. MANDARIN: Ni hao
11. RUSSIAN: Privyet
12. SPANISH: Hola
13. SWAHILI: Jambo
14. TURKISH: Merhaba
15. WELSH: Helô

LANGUAGES IN PERIL

TODAY, there are more than 7,000 languages spoken on Earth. But by 2100, more than half of those may disappear. In fact, experts say one language dies every two weeks, due to the increasing dominance of larger languages, such as English, Spanish, and Mandarin. So what can be done to keep dialects from disappearing? Efforts like National Geographic's Enduring Voices Project have been created to track and document the world's most threatened indigenous languages, such as Tofa, spoken only by people in Siberia, and Magati Ke, from Aboriginal Australia. The hope is to preserve these languages—and the cultures they belong to.

10 LEADING LANGUAGES

Approximate population of first-language speakers (in millions)

Rank	Language	Speakers
1.	Chinese*	1,299
2.	Spanish	442
3.	English	378
4.	Arabic	315
5.	Hindi	260
6.	Bengali	243
7.	Portuguese	223
8.	Russian	154
9.	Japanese	122
10.	Punjabi	93

Some languages have only a few hundred speakers, while Chinese has nearly 1.3 billion native speakers worldwide. That's about triple the next largest group of language speakers. Colonial expansion, trade, and migration account for the spread of the other most widely spoken languages. With growing use of the internet, English is becoming the language of the technology age.

*Includes all forms of the language.

6 fun language facts

1 The **most commonly** used letters in the English language are **E, T, A,** and **O.**

2 The **Russian** word for **"RED"** also means **"beautiful."**

3 The **longest** word in English is **pneumonoul-tramicroscopic-silicovolcanoco-niosis,** a lung disease.

4 Babies' **cries** can sound **different** in various **languages.**

5 People in **Papua New Guinea** speak more than **840** languages.

6 The word **"taxi"** means the same thing in English, German, French, Swedish, Spanish, and Portuguese.

TAXI

MYTHOLOGY

GREEK

EGYPTIAN

The ancient Greeks believed that many gods and goddesses ruled the universe. According to this mythology, the Olympians lived high atop Greece's Mount Olympus. Each of these 12 principal gods and goddesses had a unique personality that corresponded to particular aspects of life, such as love or death.

Egyptian mythology is based on a creation myth that tells of an egg that appeared on the ocean. When the egg hatched, out came Ra, the sun god. As a result, ancient Egyptians became worshippers of the sun and of the nine original deities, most of whom were the children and grandchildren of Ra.

THE OLYMPIANS

Aphrodite was the goddess of love and beauty.

Apollo, Zeus's son, was the god of the sun, music, and healing. Artemis was his twin.

Ares, Zeus's son, was the god of war.

Artemis, Zeus's daughter and Apollo's twin, was the goddess of the hunt and of childbirth.

Athena, born from the forehead of Zeus, was the goddess of wisdom and crafts.

Demeter was the goddess of fertility and nature.

Hades, Zeus's brother, was the god of the underworld and the dead.

Hephaestus, the son of Hera, was the god of fire.

Hera, the wife and older sister of Zeus, was the goddess of women and marriage.

Hermes, Zeus's son, was the messenger of the gods.

Poseidon, the brother of Zeus, was the god of the sea and earthquakes.

Zeus was the most powerful of the gods and the top Olympian. He wielded a thunderbolt and was the god of the sky and thunder.

THE NINE DEITIES

Geb, son of Shu and Tefnut, was the god of the earth.

Isis (Ast), daughter of Geb and Nut, was the goddess of fertility and motherhood.

Nephthys (Nebet-Hut), daughter of Geb and Nut, was protector of the dead.

Nut, daughter of Shu and Tefnut, was the goddess of the sky.

Osiris (Usir), son of Geb and Nut, was the god of the afterlife.

Ra (Re), the sun god, is generally viewed as the creator. He represents life and health.

Seth (Set), son of Geb and Nut, was the god of the desert and chaos.

Shu, son of Ra, was the god of air.

Tefnut, daughter of Ra, was the goddess of rain.

All cultures around the world have unique legends and traditions that have been passed down over generations. Many myths refer to gods or supernatural heroes who are responsible for occurrences in the world. For example, Norse mythology tells of the red-bearded Thor, the god of thunder, who is responsible for creating lightning and thunderstorms. And many creation myths, especially those from some of North America's native cultures, tell of an earth-diver represented as an animal that brings a piece of sand or mud up from the deep sea. From this tiny piece of earth, the entire world takes shape.

NORSE

ROMAN

Norse mythology originated in Scandinavia, in northern Europe. It was complete with gods and goddesses who lived in a heavenly place called Asgard that could be reached only by crossing a rainbow bridge.

While Norse mythology is lesser known, we use it every day. Most days of the week are named after Norse gods, including some of these major deities.

NORSE GODS

Balder was the god of light and beauty.

Freya was the goddess of love, beauty, and fertility.

Frigg, for whom Friday was named, was the queen of Asgard. She was the goddess of marriage, motherhood, and the home.

Heimdall was the watchman of the rainbow bridge and the guardian of the gods.

Hel, the daughter of Loki, was the goddess of death.

Loki, a shape-shifter, was a trickster who helped the gods—and caused them problems.

Skadi was the goddess of winter and of the hunt. She is often represented as "The Snow Queen."

Thor, for whom Thursday was named, was the god of thunder and lightning.

Tyr, for whom Tuesday was named, was the god of the sky and war.

Wodan, for whom Wednesday was named, was the god of war, wisdom, death, and magic.

Much of Roman mythology was adopted from Greek mythology, but the Romans also developed a lot of original myths as well. The gods of Roman mythology lived everywhere, and each had a role to play. There were thousands of Roman gods, but here are a few of the stars of Roman myths.

ANCIENT ROMAN GODS

Ceres was the goddess of the harvest and motherly love.

Diana, daughter of Jupiter, was the goddess of hunting and the moon.

Juno, Jupiter's wife, was the goddess of women and fertility.

Jupiter, the patron of Rome and master of the gods, was the god of the sky.

Mars, the son of Jupiter and Juno, was the god of war.

Mercury, the son of Jupiter, was the messenger of the gods and the god of travelers.

Minerva was the goddess of wisdom, learning, and the arts and crafts.

Neptune, the brother of Jupiter, was the god of the sea.

Venus was the goddess of love and beauty.

Vesta was the goddess of fire and the hearth. She was one of the most important of the Roman deities.

World Religions

A round the world, religion takes many forms. Some belief systems, such as Christianity, Islam, and Judaism, are monotheistic, meaning that followers believe in just one supreme being. Others, like Hinduism, Shintoism, and most native belief systems, are polytheistic, meaning that many of their followers believe in multiple gods.

All of the major religions have their origins in Asia, but they have spread around the world. Christianity, with the largest number of followers, has three divisions—Roman Catholic, Eastern Orthodox, and Protestant. Islam, with about one-fifth of all believers, has two main divisions—Sunni and Shiite. Hinduism and Buddhism account for almost another one-fifth of believers. Judaism, dating back some 4,000 years, has more than 13 million followers, less than one percent of all believers.

CHRISTIANITY

Based on the teachings of Jesus Christ, a Jew born some 2,000 years ago in the area of modern-day Israel, Christianity has spread worldwide and actively seeks converts. Followers in Switzerland (above) participate in an Easter season procession with lanterns and crosses.

BUDDHISM

Founded about 2,400 years ago in northern India by the Hindu prince Gautama Buddha, Buddhism spread throughout East and Southeast Asia. Buddhist temples have statues, such as the Mihintale Buddha (above) in Sri Lanka.

HINDUISM

Dating back more than 4,000 years, Hinduism is practiced mainly in India. Hindus follow sacred texts known as the Vedas and believe in reincarnation. During the festival of Navratri, which honors the goddess Durga, the Garba dance is performed (above).

136

Technology Meets Tradition

I t has been 1,200 years since the bishop of Rome became known as the pope. Pope Francis became the head of the Roman Catholic Church in 2013 and has embraced technology as a way to reach Catholics around the globe. He's the first pope to pose for a selfie and has more than 34 million Twitter followers.

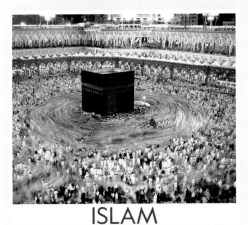

ISLAM

Muslims believe that the Koran, Islam's sacred book, records the words of Allah (God) as revealed to the Prophet Muhammad beginning around A.D. 610. Believers (above) circle the Kaaba in the Haram Mosque in Mecca, Saudi Arabia, the spiritual center of the faith.

JUDAISM

The traditions, laws, and beliefs of Judaism date back to Abraham (the Patriarch) and the Torah (the first five books of the Old Testament). Followers pray before the Western Wall (above), which stands below Islam's Dome of the Rock in Jerusalem.

137

QUIZ WHIZ

How vast is your knowledge about the world around you? Quiz yourself!

Write your answers on a piece of paper. Then check them below.

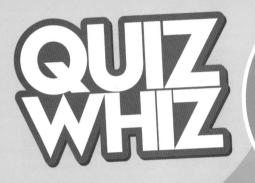

1 The word _____ means the same thing in English, German, French, Swedish, Spanish, and Portuguese.
a. "hello"
b. "goodbye"
c. "taxi"
d. "banana"

2 Today, there are more than _____ languages spoken on Earth.
a. 70
b. 700
c. 7,000
d. 70,000

3 A British artist made a dress out of _____ from around the world.
a. gum wrappers
b. postcards
c. newspapers
d. banknotes

4 _____ is a Hindu holiday often called the Festival of Lights.

5 True or false? Bell peppers are fruits, not vegetables.

Not **STUMPED** yet? Check out the *NATIONAL GEOGRAPHIC KIDS QUIZ WHIZ* collection for more crazy **CULTURE** questions!

ANSWERS: 1. c; 2. c; 3. d; 4. Diwali; 5. True

HOMEWORK HELP

Explore a New Culture

STAMPS OF BRAZIL

CURRENCY AND COINS OF BRAZIL

THE FLAG OF BRAZIL

YOU'RE A STUDENT, but you're also a citizen of the world. Writing a report on a foreign nation or your own country is a great way to better understand and appreciate how different people live. Pick the country of your ancestors, one that's been in the news, or one that you'd like to visit someday.

Passport to Success

A country report follows the format of an expository essay because you're "exposing" information about the country you choose.

The following step-by-step tips will help you with this monumental task.

1 **RESEARCH.** Gathering information is the most important step in writing a good country report. Look to internet sources, encyclopedias, books, magazine and newspaper articles, and other sources to find important and interesting details about your subject.

2 **ORGANIZE YOUR NOTES.** Put the information you gathered into a rough outline. For example, sort everything you found about the country's system of government, climate, etc.

3 **WRITE IT UP.** Follow the basic structure of good writing: introduction, body, and conclusion. Remember that each paragraph should have a topic sentence that is then supported by facts and details. Incorporate the information from your notes, but make sure it's in your own words. And make your writing flow with good transitions and descriptive language.

4 **ADD VISUALS.** Include maps, diagrams, photos, and other visual aids.

5 **PROOFREAD AND REVISE.** Correct any mistakes, and polish your language. Do your best!

6 **CITE YOUR SOURCES.** Be sure to keep a record of your sources.

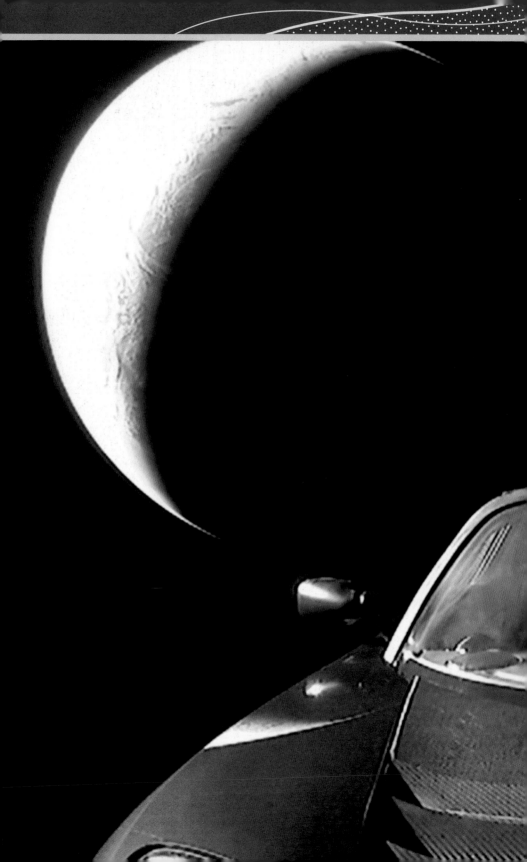

SPACE and EARTH

A Tesla roadster launched from a Falcon Heavy rocket heads around Mars with a dummy driver named "Starman" at the wheel. The Falcon Heavy—considered the world's most powerful rocket—is being tested by the company SpaceX.

EARTH EXPLORER
Meet **Christine Chen!**

This National Geographic young explorer studies ancient lakes to predict future climate change.

Just call Christine Chen a climate detective! As a geologist and climate scientist, she is on the hunt for clues about ancient climate change to piece together a puzzle that may reveal what Earth's future may look like.

So where do Christine's clues come from? She heads to ancient lake basins in places such as the Mojave Desert in California, U.S.A., and the Andes Mountains in South America. Because these specific locations are landlocked, their ancient lakes were once filled exclusively by rainfall. Over time, as the climate shifted and these landscapes went from lush and green to dry and arid, the lakes dried up—leaving behind a rocky landscape and fossilized remains of algae reefs called tufa, which Christine collects samples of and studies.

"My goal is to determine the ages of many tufa samples so that I can begin to build a broad picture of the history of lake level changes in the western United States and the central Andes," she says. "Perhaps we'll

be able to see how rainfall patterns shifted in response to past abrupt climate changes thousands of years ago."

This bigger picture, says Christine, can teach us about current climate change, including how rainfall patterns may shift as Earth's temperature rises.

"One of the biggest questions climate scientists still have is how rainfall patterns will change and reorganize in response to our rapidly warming planet," says Christine. "Will places that are already dry continue to get drier? Since water availability plays a big role in determining where people and animals can live, knowing how rainfall will change now and in the future is important."

Christine has collected tufa samples dating back to 25,000 years ago.

THE CENTRAL ANDES MOUNTAINS WHERE CHRISTINE DOES RESEARCH

" Like an archaeologist recovering artifacts from ancient human civilizations to reconstruct their history, I hunt for clues left behind by these ancient climates and try to piece together a picture of what these old climates were like. "

A CLOSE-UP LOOK AT TUFA

Some tufa towers are as a high as a three-story building.

CALL TO ACTION!

To follow Christine's rockin' career path, head to a museum to check out geology exhibits, read about local geology at your library, or simply go outside and research the rocks in your neighborhood. "Learn more about what story they capture about the history of Earth," Christine says. "Each rock on Earth has an interesting story to tell."

CHRISTINE WORKING IN THE AUSTRALIAN OUTBACK

A Universe of Galaxies

5 COOL FACTS TO RECORD

When astronauts first journeyed beyond Earth's orbit in 1968, they looked back to their home planet. The big-picture view of our place in space changed the astronauts' lives—and perhaps humanity. If you could leave the universe and similarly look back, what would you see? Remarkably, scientists are mapping this massive area. They see ... bubbles. Not literal soap bubbles, of course, but a structure that looks like of a pan full of them. Like bubble walls, thin surfaces curve around empty spaces in an elegantly simple structure. Zoom in to see that these surfaces are groups of galaxies. Zoom in further to find one galaxy, with an ordinary star—our sun—orbited by an ordinary planet—Earth. How extraordinary.

DIGITAL TRAVELER!

Take a simulated flight through our universe, thanks to the data collected by the Sloan Digital Sky Survey. Search the internet for "APOD flight through universe sdss." Sit back and enjoy the ride!

2 DARK MATTER

The universe holds a mysterious source of gravity that cannot be properly explained. This unseen matter—the ghostly dark ring in this composite Hubble telescope photo—seems to pull on galaxy clusters, drawing galaxies toward it. But what is this strange stuff? It's not giant black holes, planets, stars, or antimatter. These would show themselves indirectly. For now, astronomers call this source of gravity "dark matter."

1 GALAXY CLUSTERS AND SUPERCLUSTERS

Gravity pulls things together—gas in stars, stars in galaxies. Galaxies gather, too, sometimes by the thousands, forming galaxy clusters and superclusters with tremendously superheated gas. This gas can be as hot as 180 million degrees Fahrenheit (100 million degrees Celsius), filling space between them. These clusters hide a secret. The gravity among the galaxies isn't enough to bring them together. The source of the extra gravity is a dark secret.

3 IT STARTED WHEN ...
The Big Bang

Long ago, the universe was compressed: It was hotter, smaller, denser than now, and completely uniform—almost. Extremely minor unevenness led to a powerful energy release that astronomers call the big bang. In a blip of time, the universe expanded tremendously. The first particles formed. Atoms, galaxies, forces, and light ... all developed from this. Today's great filaments (see fact 4) may be organized where those first uneven patches existed.

4 FILAMENTS AND SHEETS
Bubbles of space

What is the universe like at its grandest scale? The biggest big-picture view is jaw-dropping. Clusters and superclusters of galaxies—red and yellow areas in this illustration—along with dark matter, string together to form structures that are millions and billions of light-years long. These so-called walls, sheets, or filaments surround vast voids, or "bubbles," of nearly empty space—the blue areas. The universe has a structure, non-random and unexpected.

5 COLLISION ZONE

Saying that galaxies form clusters and superclusters is like saying two soccer teams simply meet. During a game, there's a lot of action and energy. Similarly, as clusters and superclusters form, there's lots going on—as evidenced by the super-high-energy x-rays that are detected (pink in this colorized image).

PLANETS

MERCURY

VENUS

EARTH

MARS

CERES

JUPITER

SUN

MERCURY

Average distance from the sun:
  35,980,000 miles (57,900,000 km)
Position from the sun in orbit: 1st
Equatorial diameter: 3,030 miles (4,878 km)
Length of day: 59 Earth days
Length of year: 88 Earth days
Surface temperatures: -300°F (-184°C)
  to 800°F (427°C)
Known moons: 0
Fun fact: Mercury is shrinking.

VENUS

Average distance from the sun:
  67,230,000 miles (108,200,000 km)
Position from the sun in orbit: 2nd
Equatorial diameter: 7,520 miles (12,100 km)
Length of day: 243 Earth days
Length of year: 224.7 Earth days
Average surface temperature: 864°F (462°C)
Known moons: 0
**Fun fact: Venus is covered in thick
  clouds that reflect a lot of
  light, making it the brightest
  planet in the night sky.**

EARTH

Average distance from the sun:
  93,000,000 miles (149,600,000 km)
Position from the sun in orbit: 3rd
Equatorial diameter: 7,900 miles (12,750 km)
Length of day: 24 hours
Length of year: 365 days
Surface temperatures: -126°F (-88°C)
  to 134°F (57°C)
Known moons: 1
**Fun fact: Earth is the only planet in
  our solar system with liquid water.**

MARS

Average distance from the sun:
  141,633,000 miles (227,936,000 km)
Position from the sun in orbit: 4th
Equatorial diameter: 4,221 miles (6,794 km)
Length of day: 25 Earth hours
Length of year: 1.9 Earth years
Surface temperatures: -270°F (-168°C)
  to 80°F (27°C)
Known moons: 2
**Fun fact: Deserts have been
  discovered on Mars.**

This artwork shows the eight planets and five dwarf planets in our solar system. The relative sizes and positions of the planets are shown but not the relative distances between them.

SATURN

URANUS

NEPTUNE

PLUTO
HAUMEA
MAKEMAKE
ERIS

JUPITER

Average distance from the sun:
 483,682,000 miles (778,412,000 km)
Position from the sun in orbit: 6th
Equatorial diameter: 88,840 miles (142,980 km)
Length of day: 9.9 Earth hours
Length of year: 11.9 Earth years
Average surface temperature: -235°F (-148°C)
Known moons: 79*
Fun fact: Jupiter has a magnetic field
 that's 19,000 stronger than Earth's.

SATURN

Average distance from the sun:
 890,800,000 miles (1,433,600,000 km)
Position from the sun in orbit: 7th
Equatorial diameter: 74,900 miles (120,540 km)
Length of day: 10.7 Earth hours
Length of year: 29.5 Earth years
Average surface temperature: -218°F (-139°C)
Known moons: 62*
Fun fact: You can't walk on Saturn
 because it doesn't have a solid surface.

URANUS

Average distance from the sun:
 1,784,000,000 miles (2,871,000,000 km)
Position from the sun in orbit: 8th
Equatorial diameter: 31,760 miles (51,120 km)
Length of day: 17.2 Earth hours
Length of year: 84 Earth years
Average surface temperature: -323°F (-197°C)
Known moons: 27
Fun fact: It may rain diamonds
 on Uranus.

NEPTUNE

Average distance from the sun:
 2,795,000,000 miles (4,498,000,000 km)
Position from the sun in orbit: 9th
Equatorial diameter: 30,775 miles (49,528 km)
Length of day: 16 Earth hours
Length of year: 164.8 Earth years
Average surface temperature: -353°F (-214°C)
Known moons: 14*
Fun fact: It would take about 4,500
 years to drive to Neptune.

*Includes provisional moons, which await confirmation
 and naming from the International Astronomical Union.

For information about dwarf planets—Ceres,
Pluto, Haumea, Makemake, and Eris—see p. 148.

DWARF PLANETS

Haumea

Eris

Pluto

Thanks to advanced technology, astronomers have been spotting many never-before-seen celestial bodies with their telescopes. One new discovery? A population of icy objects orbiting the sun beyond Pluto. The largest, like Pluto itself, are classified as dwarf planets. Smaller than the moon but still massive enough to pull themselves into a ball, dwarf planets nevertheless lack the gravitational "oomph" to clear their neighborhood of other sizable objects. So, while larger, more massive planets pretty much have their orbits to themselves, dwarf planets orbit the sun in swarms that include other dwarf planets as well as smaller chunks of rock or ice.

So far, astronomers have identified five dwarf planets: Ceres, Pluto, Haumea, Makemake, and Eris. There are also three newly discovered dwarf planets that will need additional study before they are named. Astronomers are observing hundreds of newly found objects in the frigid outer solar system. As time and technology advance, the family of known dwarf planets will surely continue to grow.

CERES
Position from the sun in orbit: 5th
Length of day: 9.1 Earth hours
Length of year: 4.6 Earth years
Known moons: 0

PLUTO
Position from the sun in orbit: 10th
Length of day: 6.4 Earth days
Length of year: 248 Earth years
Known moons: 5

HAUMEA
Position from the sun in orbit: 11th
Length of day: 3.9 Earth hours
Length of year: 282 Earth years
Known moons: 2

MAKEMAKE
Position from the sun in orbit: 12th
Length of day: 22.5 Earth hours
Length of year: 305 Earth years
Known moons: 1*

ERIS
Position from the sun in orbit: 13th
Length of day: 25.9 Earth hours
Length of year: 561 Earth years
Known moons: 1

*Includes provisional moons, which await confirmation and naming from the International Astronomical Union.

THE SEARCH FOR
PLANET NINE

IS A NEPTUNE-SIZE WORLD HIDDEN IN OUR SOLAR SYSTEM?

Way out in the farthest reaches of the solar system, a mysterious undiscovered planet could be orbiting through space. It's gigantic—almost four times the size of Earth. And it's so far away that it takes up to 20,000 years to orbit the sun. Astronomers have dubbed it Planet Nine, and they're searching the skies to find it.

FAR OUT

Scientists used to think the area beyond Neptune, known as the Kuiper (sounds like KY-pur) belt, was empty. But it turns out the Kuiper belt is home to icy, rocky objects; billions of comets; and a few dwarf planets such as Pluto. While observing the belt in 2014, astronomer Mike Brown and his research partner, Konstantin Batygin, saw something strange: The orbits of many of the smaller objects in the Kuiper belt were aligned. Weirder still, they never came closer to the sun than twice the distance to Neptune. It was like something was pulling them away. But what?

STRANGE SPACE

Brown and Batygin spent over a year trying to figure out the objects' odd behavior and could only come to one conclusion. "We were convinced another planet was out there," Brown says.

To find out if they were right, the pair created a computer model illustrating the objects. Then they plugged an imaginary planet into the model. The model showed that the planet's gravity would pull on these icy objects, making them move in exactly the way they had moved in space. The pair also inferred that the planet would be roughly the size of Neptune. Like Neptune, it would likely be made of gas, and the temperature there would be a frigid minus 374.8°F (-226°C).

"It's hard to believe that we could miss something as big as Neptune!" Brown says. But the planet is really far away, about 56 billion miles (90 billion km) from Earth. If it exists, only two telescopes in the world are powerful enough to search vast areas of the sky for it efficiently—and until now, they haven't been looking for the planet.

THE HUNT IS ON

Brown and Batygin are convinced that their evidence proves that Planet Nine is hidden somewhere beyond the Kuiper belt. But Brown predicts the search will take at least a few years.

"There's this huge part of the solar system that we're only just beginning to learn about," says Brown.

OUR NEW SOLAR SYSTEM? Scientists aren't sure of Planet Nine's exact location, but they think it might lurk in the outer edges of our solar system, somewhere beyond Neptune.

SUN▶

T NINE   NEPTUNE   URANUS   SATURN   JUPITER   MARS EARTH VENUS MERCURY

Sky Calendar
2020

Jupiter

Leonid meteor shower

Supermoon

JANUARY 3–4
QUADRANTIDS METEOR SHOWER PEAK.
Featuring up to 40 meteors an hour, it is
the first meteor shower of every new year.

JANUARY 10
PENUMBRAL LUNAR ECLIPSE. Look for
the moon to darken as it passes through
Earth's penumbra—or partial shadow.
Visible throughout most of Europe, western
Australia, Asia, Africa, and the Indian
Ocean. View three more eclipses on June 5
(most of Europe, Australia, Asia, Africa, and
the Indian Ocean), July 5 (North and South
America), and November 30 (North America,
northeastern Asia, and the Pacific Ocean).

FEBRUARY 9
SUPERMOON, FULL MOON. The moon
will be full and at a close approach
to Earth, likely appearing bigger and
brighter than usual. Look for three more
supermoons on March 9, April 8, and May 7.

FEBRUARY 10
MERCURY AT GREATEST EASTERN
ELONGATION. Visible low in the western
sky just after sunset, Mercury will be
at its highest point above the horizon.

MAY 6–7
ETA AQUARIDS METEOR SHOWER PEAK.
View about 30 to 60 meteors an hour.

AUGUST 12–13
PERSEID METEOR SHOWER PEAK.
One of the best! Up to 60 meteors an
hour. Best viewing is in the direction of
the constellation Perseus.

OCTOBER 13
MARS AT OPPOSITION. Grab a friend ... and
your camera! This is your best chance to view
the red planet in 2020. Mars will appear bright
in the sky and be visible throughout the night.

OCTOBER 21–22
ORIONID METEOR SHOWER PEAK.
View up to 20 meteors an hour. Look toward
the constellation Orion for the best show.

NOVEMBER 17–18
LEONID METEOR SHOWER PEAK.
View up to 15 meteors an hour.

DECEMBER 13–14
GEMINID METEOR SHOWER PEAK.
A spectacular show! Up to 120
multicolored meteors an hour.

DECEMBER 21
RARE CONJUNCTION OF JUPITER AND
SATURN. Look for two bright planets in the
western sky just after sunset. They will be so
close they could appear as a double planet! The
last time this rare event occurred was 2000.

VARIOUS DATES THROUGHOUT 2020
VIEW THE INTERNATIONAL SPACE STATION.
Visit spotthestation.nasa.gov to find out when
the ISS will be flying over your neighborhood.

Dates may vary slightly depending on your
location. Check with a local planetarium for
the best viewing time in your area.

SUPER SUN!

THE SUN IS 99.8 PERCENT OF ALL THE MASS IN OUR SOLAR SYSTEM.

The SUN'S surface is about 10,000°F! (5500°C)

Even from 93 million miles (150 million km) away, the sun's rays are powerful enough to provide the energy needed for life to flourish on Earth. This 4.6-billion-year-old star is the anchor of our solar system and accounts for more than 99 percent of the mass in the solar system. What else makes the sun so special? For starters, it's larger than one million Earths and is the biggest object in our solar system. The sun also converts about four million tons (3,628,739 t) of matter to energy every second, helping to make life possible here on Earth. Now that's *sun*-sational!

The SUN has HOLES in it.

Storms on the Sun!

Solar flares are 10 million times more powerful than a volcanic eruption on Earth.

With the help of specialized equipment, scientists have observed solar flares—or bursts of magnetic energy that explode from the sun's surface as a result of storms on the sun. Solar storms occur about 2,000 times every 11 years, or once every two days. Most solar storms are minor and do not impact Earth. But the fiercer the flare, the more we may potentially feel its effects, as it could disrupt power grids or interfere with GPS navigation systems. Solar storms can also trigger stronger-than-usual auroras, light shows that can be seen on Earth.

Some solar storms travel at speeds of **THREE MILLION MILES AN HOUR** (4.8 million km/h).

Solar storm

ROCK STARS

The world is full of rocks—some big, some small, some formed deep within the Earth, and some formed at the surface. While they may look similar, not all rocks are created equal. Look closely, and you'll see differences between every boulder, stone, and pebble. Here's more about the three top varieties of rocks.

Igneous

Named for the Greek word meaning "from fire," igneous rocks form when hot, molten liquid called magma cools. Pools of magma form deep underground and slowly work their way to the Earth's surface. If they make it all the way, the liquid rock erupts and is called lava. As the layers of lava build up, they form a mountain called a volcano. Typical igneous rocks include obsidian, basalt, and pumice, which is so chock-full of gas bubbles that it actually floats in water.

ANDESITE

GRANITE PORPHYRY

Metamorphic

Metamorphic rocks are the masters of change! These rocks were once igneous or sedimentary, but thanks to intense heat and pressure deep within the Earth, they have undergone a total transformation from their original form. These rocks never truly melt; instead, the heat twists and bends them until their shapes substantially change. Metamorphic rocks include slate as well as marble, which is used for buildings, monuments, and sculptures.

MICA SCHIST

BANDED GNEISS

Sedimentary

When wind, water, and ice constantly wear away and weather rocks, smaller pieces called sediment are left behind. These are sedimentary rocks, also known as gravel, sand, silt, and clay. As water flows downhill, it carries the sedimentary grains into lakes and oceans, where they get deposited. As the loose sediment piles up, the grains eventually get compacted or cemented back together again. The result is new sedimentary rock. Sandstone, gypsum, limestone, and shale are sedimentary rocks that have formed this way.

LIMESTONE

HALITE

A LOOK INSIDE

The **CRUST** includes tectonic plates, landmasses, and the ocean. Its average thickness varies from 5 to 25 miles (8 to 40 km).

The **MANTLE** is about 1,800 miles (2,897 km) of hot, thick, solid rock.

The **OUTER CORE** is liquid molten lava made mostly of iron and nickel.

The **INNER CORE** is a solid center made mostly of iron and nickel.

The distance from Earth's surface to its center is 3,963 miles (6,378 km) at the Equator. There are four layers: a thin, rigid crust; the rocky mantle; the outer core, which is a layer of molten iron; and finally the inner core, which is believed to be solid iron.

What would happen if Earth had rings like Saturn?

It's good that Earth *doesn't* have rings. Saturn's rings are made of countless pieces of rock and ice that can be as tiny as a grain of sand or as big as a house. If Earth had similar rings, they'd be positioned in a way that would block sunlight and cast a shadow over the Northern and Southern Hemispheres during each region's winter. (That's when the hemispheres are tilted away from the sun.) Both areas would be darker and colder at these times. With less light coming in, crops and plants that depend on the sun to survive the season might die out. No thanks!

It's a Rocky World!

ROCKS AND MINERALS can be found in a wide range of different environments. In addition to being useful materials, they also give scientists clues to how our world has changed over time.

GRANITE Plutonic igneous rock rich in quartz and feldspar. It is a hard rock used as a building stone and for monuments.

GYPSUM Sedimentary rock that forms from the evaporation of mineral-rich water.

FOSSILS IN SHALE Shale is a fine-grained sedimentary rock made from compacted mud. It often contains fossils of extinct organisms or plants, such as the fern at right.

SANDSTONE Sedimentary rock that forms when sand grains get cemented back together again.

BASALT The most common type of igneous rock, basalts form most of the Earth's crust under the ocean.

OLIVINE This group of greenish minerals is found mainly in dark-colored igneous rocks such as basalt, peridotite, and gabbro.

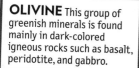

BERYL Commonly found in pegmatite and schist. Well-formed green beryl crystals are also known as emeralds.

TOURMALINE Commonly found in both igneous and metamorphic rocks.

SULFUR AND SALT CRYSTALS They give the crater of Dallol volcano in Ethiopia its unique color.

FELDSPAR Like quartz, feldspar can be found in all three major rock types.

FLUORITE Most often found in igneous and metamorphic rocks.

NATIVE COPPER This soft metal forms with basalt in hydrothermal vents near volcanoes.

A HOT TOPIC

WHAT GOES ON INSIDE A STEAMING, BREWING VOLCANO?

If you could look inside a volcano, you'd see something that looks like a long pipe, called a conduit. It leads from inside the magma chamber under the crust up to a vent, or opening, at the top of the mountain. Some conduits have branches that shoot off to the side, called fissures.

When pressure builds from gases inside the volcano, the gases must find an escape, and they head up toward the surface! An eruption occurs when lava, gases, ash, and rocks explode out of the vent.

Vent

Conduit

Fissures

Magma Chamber

TYPES OF VOLCANOES

CINDER CONE VOLCANO
Eve's Cone, Canada

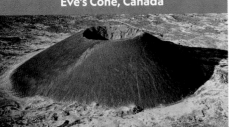

Cinder cone volcanoes look like an upside-down ice-cream cone. They spew out cinder and hot ash. Some of these volcanoes smoke and erupt for years at a time.

COMPOSITE VOLCANO
Licancábur, Chile

Composite volcanoes, or stratovolcanoes, form as lava, ash, and cinder from previous eruptions harden and build up over time. These volcanoes spit out pyroclastic flows, or thick explosions of hot ash that travel at hundreds of miles an hour.

SHIELD VOLCANO
Mauna Loa, Hawaii, U.S.A.

The gentle, broad slopes of a shield volcano look like an ancient warrior's shield. Its eruptions are often slower. Lava splatters and bubbles rather than shooting forcefully into the air.

LAVA DOME VOLCANO
Mount St. Helens, Washington, U.S.A.

Dome volcanoes have steep sides. Hardened lava often plugs the vent at the top of a dome volcano. Pressure builds beneath the surface until the top blows.

HOT SPOTS Some volcanoes form at hot spots, or holes beneath Earth's crust in the middle of a tectonic plate. As lava pushes up through the hole and forms a volcanic island, the plate keeps moving. More volcanoes form as it moves. Some hot spots are big enough to create a chain of volcanic islands, such as the Hawaiian Islands.

COLLAPSE! An erupting volcano can cause damage to itself! A caldera is a large bowl-like depression caused by the collapse of a magma chamber during an eruption. Crater Lake in Oregon, U.S.A., is a caldera that has filled with rainwater and snowfall.

FROZEN

A COLORFUL ICE CAVE LIES HIDDEN BENEATH A REMOTE RUSSIAN GLACIER.

RUSSIA

Bering Sea

Kamchatka Peninsula

Sea of Okhotsk

KAMCHATKA CAVE

PACIFIC OCEAN

RUSSIA

NORTH AMERICA

ASIA

PACIFIC OCEAN

The inside of Kamchatka (Kam-CHAT-kuh) Cave is full of cool shades of white and gray. That's because it's an ice cave—a 20-foot (6-m)-high, 30-foot (9-m)-wide passage that tunnels half a mile (0.8 km) through a glacier. But sometimes the cave's scenery is transformed. Its icy interior occasionally glows with a dazzling display of blue and violet lights. So what gives this cave its unique colors?

COLD HARD FACTS

The icy tunnel is tucked away in a remote valley on the Kamchatka Peninsula in Russia. But because it's a three-hour off-road drive from the nearest community, the cave was hidden from the world until 2012. That's when local hiking guide Denis Budkov and some fellow adventurers discovered the site.

The magical-looking cave is in a region known for a weird mix of volcanoes and glaciers.

That's why Kamchatka is sometimes called "the land of fire and ice." It's a combination of these two forces that created the cavern.

The first force in action: ice. Regular winter blizzards in the area created gigantic snow piles, which eventually became the many glaciers found on Kamchatka. "The weight of the snow from above squeezes ice crystals together," says Daniel McGrath, a glacier scientist with the U.S. Geological Survey. "Over long periods of time, these crystals combine to produce a glacier." Or, in this case, hundreds of glaciers.

But how did one of these glaciers become an ice cave? Blame the second force, fire—sort of. A nearby volcano-heated spring sends a steady stream of hot water down a mountainside that the glacier runs up against. Steam from this water seeped under the glacier and hollowed it out from the ground up, carving out the ice cave.

WORLD

Russia is the world's largest country. It covers about 11 percent of Earth's land.

THE ENTRANCE TO THE CAVE IS ONLY ACCESSIBLE TO EXPERIENCED HIKERS.

The Ural Mountains split Russia between two continents, Europe and Asia.

The country's Trans-Siberian Railway, the world's longest railroad, stretches from Europe to the Sea of Japan.

THIS IS A PERSON!

THE RED COLOR OF A FLARE REFLECTS OFF THE CAVE'S INTERIOR, GIVING AN EXPLORER A BETTER VIEW.

RAINBOW ROOF

The colors visible in the cave's ceiling are a result of sunlight streaming in through the cave's thin walls—or, at least, trying to. Snow and ice have something called a high albedo, meaning they reflect much of the sunlight that reaches their surface. But some shades of light are able to filter through water better than others. Red and yellow hues don't make it very far through the cave's icy ceiling, but blue and violet shades do.

MAJOR MELTDOWN

Some melting is natural for glaciers. Budkov has witnessed this meltdown in Kamchatka, where the area of the peninsula's visible glaciers has shrunk

TAKE A PEEK INTO KAMCHATKA CAVE'S ICY INTERIOR. The water in the cave's stream comes from a hot spring gushing from the nearby Mutnovsky volcano and winds about a half mile (0.8 km) until it dries up at the cave's end. Sunlight streaming into the cavern through the glacial ice that forms the "roof" of the cave creates spectacular light shows on the inside.

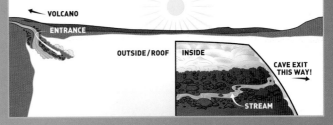

VOLCANO

ENTRANCE

OUTSIDE / ROOF   INSIDE

CAVE EXIT THIS WAY!

STREAM

by about 24 percent since 2000. But even though Kamchatka Cave has melted a couple of times, it always reforms. "If it melts, it reappears the next year," Budkov says. Guess you could call it the comeback cave.

QUIZ WHIZ

Are your space and Earth smarts out of this world? Take this quiz!

Write your answers on a piece of paper. Then check them below.

1 **True or false?** There will be 14 supermoon sightings in 2020.

2 **What is Earth's outer core made of?**
a. mud
b. molten lava
c. minerals
d. marshmallows

3 **True or false?** The sun has holes in it.

4 **Which of the following is NOT a volcano?**
a. lava dome
b. composite
c. shield
d. sedimentary

5 **_____ is an example of metamorphic rock.**
a. Marble
b. Pumice
c. Brick
d. Limestone

Not **STUMPED** yet? Check out the *NATIONAL GEOGRAPHIC KIDS QUIZ WHIZ* collection for more crazy **SPACE AND EARTH** questions!

ANSWERS:
1. False. There will be four supermoons in 2020; 2. b; 3. True; 4. d; 5. a

HOMEWORK HELP

ACE YOUR SCIENCE FAIR

You can learn a lot about science from books, but to really experience it firsthand, you need to get into the lab and "do" some science. Whether you're entering a science fair or just want to learn more on your own, there are many scientific projects you can do. So put on your goggles and lab coat, and start experimenting.

Most likely, the topic of the project will be up to you. So remember to choose something that is interesting to you.

THE BASIS OF ALL SCIENTIFIC INVESTIGATION AND DISCOVERY IS THE SCIENTIFIC METHOD. CONDUCT YOUR EXPERIMENT USING THESE STEPS:

Observation/Research—Ask a question or identify a problem.

Hypothesis—Once you've asked a question, do some thinking and come up with some possible answers.

Experimentation—How can you determine if your hypothesis is correct? You test it. You perform an experiment. Make sure the experiment you design will produce an answer to your question.

Analysis—Gather your results, and use a consistent process to carefully measure the results.

Conclusion—Do the results support your hypothesis?

Report Your Findings—Communicate your results in the form of a paper that summarizes your entire experiment.

Bonus!

Take your project one step further. Your school may have an annual science fair, but there are also local, state, regional, and national science fair competitions. Compete with other students for awards, prizes, and scholarships!

EXPERIMENT DESIGN

There are three types of experiments you can do.

MODEL KIT—a display, such as an "erupting volcano" model. Simple and to the point.

DEMONSTRATION—shows the scientific principles in action, such as a tornado in a wind tunnel.

INVESTIGATION—the home run of science projects, and just the type of project for science fairs. This kind demonstrates proper scientific experimentation and uses the scientific method to reveal answers to questions.

KNOCK, KNOCK.

Who's there?
T. rex
T. rex who?
There's a T. rex at your door and you want to know its name?